AF600667

THE CATHOLIC UNIVERSITY OF AMERICA
Canon Law Studies
No. 301

THE PLACE FOR THE HEARING OF CONFESSIONS

A HISTORICAL SYNOPSIS AND A COMMENTARY

by

REV. FRANCIS J. FAZZALARO, A. B., J. C. L.
Priest of the Diocese of Hartford

A DISSERTATION

Submitted to the Faculty of the School of Canon Law of the Catholic University of America in Partial Fulfillment of the Requirements for the Degree of Doctor of Canon Law

THE CATHOLIC UNIVERSITY OF AMERICA PRESS
WASHINGTON, D. C.
1950

Nihil obstat:
HIERONYMUS D. HANNAN, A. M., S. T. D., LL. B., J. C. D.
Censor Deputatus

Washingtonii, D. C., die 5 augusti 1949

Imprimatur:
✠ HENRICUS J. O'BRIEN, D. D.
Episcopus Hartfordiensis

Hartfordiae, die 19 augusti 1949

PRINTED IN THE UNITED STATES OF AMERICA
BY ST. ANTHONY GUILD PRESS, PATERSON, N. J.

IN GRATITUDE TO HIS EXCELLENCY
THE MOST REVEREND HENRY J. O'BRIEN
BISHOP OF HARTFORD

TABLE OF CONTENTS

Part One — HISTORICAL SYNOPSIS

FOREWORD

Sancta sancte tractanda has been the Church's axiomatic watchword for two thousand years in the administration of the sacraments. Since they are a sacred trust left by Christ, the Church treats these sublime gifts as it would treat the Divine Giver Himself. The greater the risk and danger of profanation or irreverence in the administration of a particular sacrament, the greater has been the Church's vigilance in regard to that sacrament. This has been especially true in regard to the sacrament of penance.

In a matter of such delicate nature, in which the frailties and weaknesses of human nature are necessarily involved, the inherent dangers are readily apparent. In setting down rules concerning the hearing of confessions, the Church has had to keep a middle course. On the one hand it had to do everything in its power to safeguard the seal of confession by veiling the act of confession with the greatest secrecy. And in this regard the Church could never be over-cautious. But, on the other hand, in view of the dangers inherent in this most delicate process, the Church was most desirous to protect both the confessor and the penitent. Thus it tried to make the act of confessing as open and public as possible.

It is a compliment to the ingenuity of the Church to see how it treated this paradox, the necessity of attaching an open and public character to an act which in its intimate nature must also remain secret. It is hard to realize that there was a time when the confessional, which is the perfect solution of the dilemma, did not exist. But a truth it is that the confessional is of comparatively recent origin, having been introduced by St. Charles Borromeo in the latter half of the sixteenth century. However, though the ideal envisions the hearing of all confessions in a confessional, it is quite apparent that that ideal is physically unachievable, for sickness and other necessary reasons immediately demand an exception.

It is the purpose of this work to consider the place in which confessions have been and must be heard, and also what rules have been set down as necessary precautions in regard to the administration of the sacrament both in and outside the confessional. The broader question of jurisdiction, that is, of the granting of faculties to hear confessions in a particular place or locality, has been left completely untouched. This work contemplates the case of a confessor who possesses the necessary faculties and permission, and attempts to determine just where he may or may not, both lawfully and validly, hear the confessions of the faithful, whether man or woman, religious or lay.

The writer wishes to express his gratitude to the Most Rev. Henry J. O'Brien, D. D., Bishop of Hartford, for the opportunity to pursue advanced studies in Canon Law; to the Faculty of the School of Canon Law of The Catholic University of America for their guidance and direction; and to all others who have in any way, by interest and by active aid, contributed to the preparation of this dissertation.

PART ONE

HISTORICAL SYNOPSIS

CHAPTER I

THE PLACE FOR THE HEARING OF CONFESSIONS UNTIL 1576

ARTICLE 1. *Secret Confession*

It is a matter of Catholic doctrine that secret confession, sacramental in character, has continued as a practice of the Church from the earliest days of Christianity. The Council of Trent stated this in the fifth chapter of the fourteenth session:

> As regards the method of confessing secretly to the priest alone, though Christ has not forbidden that one may in expiation for his crimes and for his own humiliation, for an example to others as well as for the edification of the Church thus scandalized, confess his sins publicly, yet this is not commanded by divine precept; nor would it be very prudent to enjoin by any human law that offenses, especially secret ones, should be divulged by a public confession. Wherefore, since secret sacramental confession, which holy Church has used from the beginning and still uses, has always been recommended by the most holy and ancient Fathers with great and unanimous agreement, the empty calumny of those who do not fear to teach that it [secret confession] is foreign to the divine command, is of human origin and owes its existence to the Fathers assembled in the Lateran Council, is convincingly disproved.[1]

Even though primitive texts made infrequent mention of secret confession, its existence is certain. The omission of its mention by the early writers was not without a reason. Batiffol (1861-1929) agreed with the simple but logical explanation given by Vacandard (1849-1927), namely, that secret confession was considered of secondary importance among the early Christians, since they placed the emphasis

1. Schroeder, *Canons and Decrees of the Council of Trent: Original Text with English Translation* (St. Louis: B. Herder Book Co., 1941), p. 94.

on the consequences of this confession, that is, the public penance which was performed.[2]

Since this was so, one cannot expect to find the question of the place for the hearing of confessions treated at any great length, if at all. Just what provisions were made as regards the place for hearing confessions is a question that has become largely involved in doubt and obscurity. Yet André (1809-1880), a non-Catholic scholar, in discussing from an architectural point of view medieval confessionals in England, found no difficulty in admitting that the Church, which made thorough provisions for the carrying out of its various rites, most probably also must have made provisions as to the place for the hearing of confessions, since there was an obligation incumbent on all the faithful to confess at least once a year,[3] and "an ordinance of so much importance and at the same time of so delicate a nature, should . . . have required some external means for its due and reverent performance."[4]

ARTICLE 2. *The Place for the Hearing of Confessions before the Use of Confessionals*

A. EARLY RITUALS AND PENITENTIALS

The early Rituals and Penitentials occupied themselves with indicating the questions the confessor was to ask the penitent, the works of satisfaction that were to be imposed according to the number and gravity of the penitent's faults, words of counsel, and the prayers to be recited. If they were silent on other matters it was simply for the reason that these were so well known by all as to be practiced generally.

2. Batiffol, *Etudes d'Histoire et de Théologie Positive* (Paris: V. Lecoffre, 1902), p. 212.

3. Compulsory confession did not first become the rule in the Church with the decree *Omnis utriusque sexus* of the IV Lateran Council (1215), as André seems to imply. This Council did not legislate that the faithful should confess, for this was recognized as of divine law and necessary. Rather, it decreed that the precept of confession should be complied with by all the faithful at least once a year when they had attained the age of discretion.

4. André, "Medieval Confessionals in England," *Reliquary* (London, 1860-1909), XXIV (1883-1884), 129.

Proof of the fact that confessions were heard in church before the altar is to be found in the formula of confession as contained in the Penitential usually ascribed to Egbert, Archbishop of York (735-766), composed in 735, which began thus: "I confess to Almighty God, Creator of Heaven and Earth, in the presence of this holy altar and in the presence of these precious relics which are in this holy place."[5] This same formula is also found in a manuscript of the Cathedral of St. Gatien of Tours, which dates back to the end of the ninth or the beginning of the tenth century.[6] Martène (1654-1739) made a reference to the Fifty-sixth Opusculum of St. Peter Damian (1006-1072), in which the latter spoke of having heard the confession of the Empress Agnes (1020-1077) "under the secret confession of St. Peter, before the holy altar," and another reference to Berthold (+1142), Abbot of the monastery of Garsten of the Order of Citeaux, who had the practice of hearing confessions before the altar of St. Peter.[7]

The *Liber de Divinis Officiis,* attributed to Alcuin (ca. 730-804) in the eighth century,[8] mentioned that the confessor was to make the penitent sit down at his side, and further seemed to indicate that confessions were heard either in the narthex, or in the sacristy, or in some other place connected with the church. That they generally were heard in the church itself is an incontrovertible fact. Later, from other sources, it will be seen that this was done before the altar, and as far as nuns were concerned, even in the presence of witnesses.

The *Penitential of Angers,* dating from the end of the eleventh century, ordered the penitent to rise after the preliminary general confession of guilt, which the penitent made on his knees, and then to sit together with the confessor in a secret place.[9] Inasmuch as confessions

---

5. Quoted in Morin, *Commentarius Historicus de Disciplina in Administratione Sacramenti Poenitentiae* (Venetiis: N. Pezzana, 1702), p. 570 (hereafter cited *Commentarius Historicus*).

6. Quoted in Martène, *Tractatus de Antiquis Ecclesiae Ritibus Libri Quatuor* (3 vols., Rotomagi: G. Behourt, 1700-1702), Lib. I, Cap. VI, Art. 7, Ord. 3, T. II, 50 (hereafter cited *Tractatus de Ritibus*).

7. Martène, *Tractatus de Ritibus,* Lib. IV, Pars 2a, Art. 3, Ord. 8, 16-17.

8. Migne, *Patrologiae Cursus Completus, Series Latina* (221 vols., Parisiis: 1844-1864), CI, 1196-1199.

9. "Jubeat eum surgere et sedeant pariter in secreto loco." — Morin, *Commentarius Historicus,* p. 587.

at that time were more lengthy, since they were less frequently made, the penitent did not kneel, but rather sat.

B. PRE-TRIDENTINE LOCAL CONCILIAR LEGISLATION

1) Ninth Century

The Provincial Council of Aix-la-Chapelle (816) prescribed that the confessions of nuns were to be heard in church, in plain sight of all. If sickness made it necessary, they could confess at home. But the priest had to take along with him a deacon and a subdeacon as witnesses who could testify that he had conducted himself properly.[10] The legislation was substantially repeated by the VI Council of Paris (829).[11] It stated that the confessions of nuns were to be heard only in a church, before the altar and in the presence of witnesses. If some infirmity prevented the confession from being made in a church, it was to be made in any house, but not unless witnesses were present.

2) Twelfth Century

The paucity of early legislation concerning the place for hearing confessions is attested by the fact that the next conciliar legislation comes only from 1198. In that year, Odo, Bishop of Paris (1196-1208), decreed in his *Synodal Constitutions*[12] that for the hearing of confessions priests should choose "a more common place" in the church, so that they could be seen by all. Furthermore, no priest was to hear confessions in hidden places or outside the church, except in cases of great necessity or infirmity.

10. Cap. XXVII: "Si qua [sanctimonialis] igitur peccata sua sacerdoti confiteri voluerit id in ecclesia faciat, ut ab aliis videatur, sicut in dictis sanctorum patrum continctur; exceptis infirmis, quibus in domibus id facere necesse est. Nam presbyter diaconum et subdiaconum, qui utique boni sint testimonii, ob detractionem vitandum secum habeat, a quibus scilicet videatur, et suae innocentiae bonum testimonium exhibeatur." — Mansi, *Sacrorum Conciliorum Nova et Amplissima Collectio* (53 vols. in 60, Paris-Leipzig-Arnhem, 1901-1927), XIV, 276 (hereafter cited Mansi); cf. also *Monumenta Germaniae Historica,* Legum Sectio III, *Concilia,* Tom. II, Pars II (ed. A. Werminghoff, Hannoverae et Lipsiae, 1908), 455.

11. Cap. XLVI — Mansi, XIV, 565-566.

12. Cap. VI, n. 2 — Mansi, XXII, 678.

3) *Thirteenth Century*

Many local councils in the thirteenth century considered the question. The *Constitutions of Richard Poore* (1217)[13] dealt with the problem of women's confessions, and commanded that they were to be heard *extra velum*. This veil was known in England and France as the "Lenten Veil" or "Curtain," and in Germany as the "Hunger Cloth." During the Lenten season it was used to veil off the sanctuary from the faithful until Wednesday of Holy Week when in the Passion were read the words *Velum templi scissum est*. It was a sort of fiction of law, symbolic in nature. Just as Christians by the reception of ashes on Ash Wednesday avowedly became penitents, so too their exclusion from the church, which had been an important part of the old rigorous canonical penitential discipline, was indicated by this veil which hung across the arch of the chancel, since figuratively they could be regarded as being outside the church. In the ordinary parish churches the veil was suspended between the chancel and the nave. In the cathedrals, however, it shrouded only the sanctuary, and the monks or canons in choir took their places outside the curtain.[14]

In requiring, then, that the confessions of women be heard outside this Lenten veil, the Provincial Council's constitution was attempting to give extreme publicity and prominence to the act of confession in order to safeguard proper decorum. It added the explanation, however, that the confessor and penitent were to be seen, not heard. Therefore the place was not to be within earshot of anyone, but merely in plain view. St. Edmund Rich, Archbishop of Canterbury (1233-1240), passed the same regulation in his *Provincial Constitutions* (1236).[15]

The Provincial Council of Narbonne (1227)[16] and the Council of Trier (1227)[17] both were content with the general statement that those who heard confessions should do so in an open and not in an occult

13. Cap. XXV — Mansi, XXII, 1115.
14. Thurston, *Lent and Holy Week* (New York: Longmans, Green and Co., 1904), pp. 99-100, 103.
15. Cap. XVII — Mansi, XXIII, 421; cf. also Council of Oxford (1222), Cap. XLI, *De Poenitentia* — Mansi, XXII, 1176.
16. Cap. VII — Mansi, XXIII, 23.
17. Cap. IV — Mansi, XXIII, 28.

place. The Diocesan Synod of Rouen (1235)[18] required a *locus eminens,* which can best be understood as an elevated or high place, one that easily stood out. The Council of Béziers (1246)[19] demanded an open place, not one that was occult. In the same year the Synodal Statutes of a certain Bishop Richard[20] forbade the confessions of women except *extra velum.* In the next year the Synodal Statutes of the Diocese of Le Mans[21] decreed that for confessions priests were to choose some elevated place (*locus eminens*) that they might be seen *communiter,* that is, by all. The Synodal Constitutions of the Diocese of Valence (1255)[22] ordered priests, when hearing confessions, to select a convenient place, but one which would allow them to be seen by everyone in church. They were to hear confessions outside the church only in cases of great necessity or sickness.

The Council of Mainz (1261)[23] stated specifically that the reason why some elevated place in church should be chosen, when the priest sat to hear confessions, was to obviate all suspicion. The Council of Trier (1277)[24] merely required an open place.

John Peckham, Archbishop of Canterbury (1279-1292), issued an Edict (1279) for the reformation of nuns. This is often given as an appendix to the Council of Reading.[25] He made an important addition to the legislation of his predecessor, already mentioned above, by invalidating the absolution given by any priest to a penitent whose confession had not been heard in a public place, exposed to all passersby: *Circa confessiones autem taliter duximus ordinandum: ut in loco tantum fiant publico, coram altari, exposito transeuntibus universis: nec valet absolutio secus facta.* One could possibly question the power of the ordinary to add such an invalidating clause to his statute. However, it was entirely within his power to grant jurisdiction to confessors and to base the valid use of that jurisdiction on a condition, even

18. Cap. LXXXIII — Mansi, XXIII, 387.
19. Cap. XLVI — Mansi, XXIII, 704.
20. *De Poenitentia* — Mansi, XXIII, 705.
21. *De Confessione et Poenitentia* — Mansi, XXIII, 737; cf. also Synod of Clermont (1268), Cap. VII — Mansi, XXIII, 1194.
22. *De Confessione* — Mansi, XXIII, 888.
23. Cap. VIII — Mansi, XXIII, 1082.
24. Cap. IV — Mansi, XXIV, 195.
25. Mansi, XXIV, 266.

though as in this case that condition be indicated only implicitly. Thus in effect he could say: "I grant you jurisdiction to hear confessions, provided that the place in which you hear them is public, before the altar, and open to the view of passersby." Thus in cases in which the confessor did not fulfill these conditions the ordinary actually withheld jurisdiction, so that the confession if heard apart from the fulfillment of these conditions was invalid because of the confessor's lack of jurisdiction.

The Synod of Cologne (1280)[26] held under Archbishop Sigfried (1275-1297) decreed that priests should for the hearing of confessions choose a place in the church that was common and apt, so that they could be seen by all; they were not to hear confessions in obscure or dark places, or outside the church, except in cases of great necessity or infirmity. The Synod further decreed that all violators of this decree would be *ipso facto* excommunicated: *Contrarium facientes sententiam excommunicationis se noverint incursuros.* It is also interesting to note that the same Synod commanded that priests should not hear confessions before sunrise or after sundown, except in cases of great necessity, and then only in a well-lighted place in the presence of witnesses. Moreover, a priest was not to hear the confession of a woman when she was alone in church. If he disobeyed, he was *ipso facto* excommunicated, and had to fast for three days on bread and water.

The Synod of Liège (1287)[27] contained substantially the same legislation as the Synod of Cologne (1280), with the important exception, however, that it omitted mention of any penal sanctions.

The Provincial Council of Nîmes (1298)[28] passed the following statute, important because it made specific provision in the event that confessions could not be heard in church:

> In confessionibus magnam adhibeant diligentiam sacerdotes, et confessiones audiant in ecclesia ut ab omnibus valeant intueri: et ubi non erit ecclesia, utputa in casali, non in camera vel gardaroba, sed in cappella si fuerit, vel in palatio, seu in alio loco non suspecto, nisi necessitas aliud suaderet.

---

26. Cap. VIII — Mansi, XXIV, 353.
27. Cap. IV — Mansi, XXIV, 890-891; cf. also Synod of Exeter (1287), Cap. V — Mansi, XXIV, 790.
28. Cap. IV — Mansi, XXVI, 349.

If confessions were to be heard at a summer villa, for example, they were not to be heard in a room or in a cloakroom, but in the chapel, if one was available, or in the courtyard or some other open place that would not lead to suspicion, except when necessity demanded that he proceed otherwise.[29]

4) *Fourteenth Century*

The Statutes of the Diocese of Nevers (1300)[30] furnish an interesting point for observation. Priests were commanded to select for confessions an open place, so that they could be seen by all, and were not to hear confessions *in locis editis* or outside the church. In many of the diocesan statutes already mentioned, this same decree is had practically verbatim, except for the word *editis,* which in the others is supplanted with *abditis.* Whether a manuscript or printing error is responsible for this difference is a matter of conjecture. It must be admitted, however, that the better meaning — if not the only logical one — is found in the word *abditis.* It is also worthy of note that the only provision made by the Synod for deviation from the general rule which it set down was in cases of especially great (*praemaxima*) necessity. Most of the other synods were content to make exceptions in case of any necessity.

In the same year 1300, two other Synods, Constance[31] and Bayeux,[32] passed statutes differing from that of the Synod of Nevers only in respect to the two points just mentioned. The Council of Lambeth (1330)[33] decreed that confessions, especially those of women, were not to be heard in hidden places in the church. Exception was made only in cases of very great (*maxima*) necessity or of infirmity on the part of the penitent.

The Constitutions of the Synod of Padua (1339)[34] expressly included regular as well as secular priests in its prohibition from hearing confessions in the corners or occult places in churches. The confessions of women who were not ill were not to be received in any place but in

29. Cf. Synod of Würzburg, Cap. XXI — Mansi, XXIV, 1196.
30. Mansi, XXXII, 293.
31. Cap. XXXIV — Mansi, XXV, 38.
32. Cap. LXXXI — Mansi, XXV, 75.
33. Cap. II — Mansi, XXV, 892.
34. Cap. IX — Mansi, XXV, 1136.

the church itself. In the case of sick women the confessor was commanded to use only such a place as would enable both him and the penitent to be seen not only by other women in the house of the sick person, but also by a male companion of the priest, whom, apparently, the statute implicitly required him to take along. It cautioned, however, that these witnesses should be removed far enough, so as not to be able to overhear the confession. Failure to obey this statute would result in a fine.[35]

The Council of Prague (1346)[36] merely made the general statement that confessions were to be heard in church. And the Constitutions of the Diocese of Lugano (1351)[37] expressly allowed priests to enter the cloister to hear the confession of a nun in danger of death.

5) *Fifteenth Century*

None of the provincial councils or diocesan synods which were held during the fifteenth century and whose decrees are contained in Mansi's collection passed any statutes regarding the place for the hearing of confessions.

6) *Sixteenth Century*

The Synodal Statutes (1508) of Wary de Dommartin, Bishop of Verdun,[38] required priests in hearing confessions to choose an elevated place, one not behind the altar, in order to be seen easily. They provided that only in cases of great necessity or of infirmity could confessions be heard outside the church.

The Council of Manfredonia (1567)[39] explicitly forbade confessions to be heard in the sacristy. The following year the Council of Ravenna,[40] in forbidding the confessions of women to be heard out-

---

35. This was a fine of a certain amount of wax, twenty pounds in this case, rather than money. For examples of such fines, cf. Bizzarri, *Collectanea in Usum Secretariae S. Congregationis Episcoporum et Regularium* (Romae, 1885), pp. 340, 342 (hereafter cited *Collectanea*).

36. *De Poenitentiis et Remissionibus* — Mansi, XXVI, 101.

37. Cap. LVI — Mansi, XXVI, 278.

38. Quoted by Dom Chardon in Migne, *Theologiae Cursus Completus* (28 vols., Parisiis, 1839-1845), II, 734.

39. *De Poenitentia* — Mansi, XXXV B, 879.

40. Cap. II — Mansi, XXXV A, 619-620.

side the confessional seat in church without necessity, also provided a penalty to be imposed according to the will of the bishop. The Council of Florence (1573)[41] likewise imposed a similar penalty for the same infraction.

The Council of Genoa (1574)[42] strongly condemned and abrogated the custom in vogue in some places whereby confessors went about hearing confessions from door to door in the cities, towns, and villages.

C. CONFESSIONS OF THE SICK

A priori it is not difficult to imagine that in the case of sick persons their confessions, naturally enough, were heard in the very room in which their illness confined them. To exact of them anything further would have been to demand the physically impossible. Though the *Corpus Iuris Canonici* did not consider the question of the place for the hearing of confessions, nevertheless Gregory IX (1227-1241) did mention in the Decretals that the confessions of the sick should be heard in the very sick-room.

> Quum infirmitas corporalis nonnumquam ex peccato proveniat, dicente Domino languido, quem sanaverat: "Vade, et amplius noli peccare, ne deterius aliquid tibi contingat," praesenti decreto statuimus et districte praecipimus medicis corporum, ut, quum eos ad infirmos vocari contigerit, ipsos ante omnia moneant et inducant, ut medicos advocent animarum, ut, postquam fuerit infirmo de spirituali salute provisum, ad corporalis medicinae remedium salubrius procedatur, quum causa cessante cesset effectus. Hoc quidem inter alia huic causam dedit edicto, quod quidem, in aegritudinis lecto iacentes, quum eis a medicis suadetur, ut de animarum salute disponant, in desperationis articulum incidunt, unde facilius mortis periculum incurrunt. . . .[43]

If the "doctor of the soul" was to be called in to administer to the patient's spiritual needs, would not the foremost among these needs have been confession?

---

41. Cap. III — Mansi, XXXV A, 762.
42. Cap. X, n. 3 — Mansi, XXXVI bis, 574.
43. C. 13, X, *de poenitentiis et remissionibus,* V, 38.

The II Council of Ravenna (1311)[44] warned doctors, when called to a patient's bedside, not to return to care for him, unless it was clear that the sick person had called in the spiritual doctor (priest) to administer first to the needs of his soul. If any doctor held this warning in contempt and disobeyed it, he was to be denied entrance into the church until such time as, in the judgment of the ordinary, he had made ample satisfaction for his transgression.

A council which was held in Spain in the year 1512[45] explicitly stated that the "doctors of souls" to be notified by the physicians were confessors, who were to try to induce the patient to go to confession.

The Council of Magdeburg (1489)[46] strongly commanded that, inasmuch as very often it happened that the sick were ashamed to confess their sins on account of the number of people who were present, confessors were to hear their confessions in an informal and secret manner.

The numerous local conciliar decrees already cited also expressly mentioned very frequently that an exception to the rule of hearing confessions in church, especially those of women, was to be made in cases of infirmity.[47]

D. CONFESSION BY MESSENGER AND BY LETTER

The question of confession by messenger and by letter was considered, though briefly, in the *Decree of Gratian.* In arguing for the necessity of presenting oneself before the priest in order to receive sacramental absolution, Gratian recalled how Christ commanded the cleansed lepers to show themselves to the priest. He did not allow simply one of them to go to the priest and to act in behalf of the others. Therefore Gratian concluded that corporal presence was necessary, and

---

44. Mansi, XXV, 458.

45. Mansi, XXXII, 584-585.

46. Mansi, XXXII, 491; cf. also Provincial Council of Fritzlar (1246), Mansi, XXIII, 726; Council of Mainz (1310), *De Confessionibus Audiendis* — Mansi, XXV, 345.

47. Cf. Synodal Statutes of Odo (1198), Cap. VI, n. 2 — Mansi, XXII, 678; Synod of Valence (1255), *De Confessione* — Mansi, XXIII, 888; Synod of Cologne (1280), Cap. VIII — Mansi, XXIV, 353; Council of Lambeth (1330), Cap. II — Mansi, XXV, 892.

that it was not enough either to be represented by a messenger, or to write a letter. He said:

> Praecepit enim Dominus mundandis, ut ostenderent ora sacerdotibus, docens corporali praesentia confitenda peccata, non per nuntium, non per scriptum manifestanda. Dixit enim "Ora monstrate" et "Omnes" non unus pro omnibus: non alium statuatis nuntium, qui pro vobis offerat munus a Moyse statutum: sed qui per vos peccastis, per vos erubescatis. Erubescentia enim ipsa partem habet remissionis. Ex misericordia enim hoc praecepit Dominus, ut neminem poeniteret in occulto. In hoc enim, quod per seipsum dicit sacerdoti, et erubescentiam vincit timore offensi, fit venia criminis.[48]

ARTICLE 3. *The Introduction of Confessionals in 1576*

A. REGULATIONS OF ST. CHARLES BORROMEO

The confessional as it is known today was originated in its basic and essential elements by St. Charles Borromeo, Archbishop of Milan (1565-1584). In the IV Provincial Council of Milan (1576) he decreed that every parochial church was to have a confessional constructed according to the form described in his "Book of Instructions."[49] Up until that time such a device was entirely unknown, as can be seen easily from the conciliar decrees and other sources already mentioned. Theretofore it was generally required that there be simply a confessional seat located in some convenient but open place in the church. Various terms were used to describe the location, but all were concerned primarily with the fact that it be open to public view, and that it be not situated in a dark or hidden place. It was especially imperative that the confessions of women should not be heard outside such a place in the church, especially not in rooms or in private homes. The only two exceptions were to be made in cases of illness or infirmity and necessity. Occasionally, for violations of these requirements, penal sanctions were invoked either in that the confession itself was rendered null and void, or in that the confessor was punished with excommunication, suspension, or the imposition of a fine.

---

48. C. 88, D. I, *de poenit.*

49. Borromeo, *Acta Ecclesiae Mediolanensis* (2 vols., Lugduni, 1682-3), I, 11 (hereafter cited *Acta*).

St. Charles embodied in his legislation regarding the place for the hearing of confessions all the essential elements of previous conciliar decrees. In addition he devised many specific details and regulations of his own. In the I Provincial Council of Milan (1565), he had merely followed the general pattern of the numerous decrees already cited. It may be mentioned here that he seemed somewhat strict in not permitting even the confessions of men, and *a fortiori* those of women, to be heard in private homes when there was not some necessary reason.[50] But then, in 1576, this great reformer ordered in his archdiocese the use of confessionals, whose construction he had so minutely described in his "Book of Instructions."[51] It was he, in fact, who gave the confessional its very name. The following is a minute description of the newly invented confessional.

It was to be entirely constructed of walnut or some other wood and, as long as it followed the necessary requirements, it could be elaborately ornamented. It was to be closed on three sides, that is, on the left, on the right, and at the back, and also covered on top, but entirely open in front. However, in the more frequented churches it could have a trellis-work door or wooden bars which left openings of about four inches,[52] or also a door which closed with a lock so that no one other than the confessor could enter. St. Charles mentioned the reasons for having the confessional locked whenever the confessor did not occupy it. The locking of the confessional would prevent laymen, vagrants, and evil-intentioned men from sitting in it or perhaps also falling asleep in it.

---

50. Borromeo, *Acta,* I, 113; cf. also Mansi, XXXIV A, 22.

51. Borromeo, *Acta,* I, 485-6.

52. *Uncia,* according to St. Charles' own explanation (cf. *Acta,* 1, 386, 531, 588), was the smallest division of a cubit (*cubitum*), which in turn was composed of twenty-four *unciae.* However, because the sample measurements which he gave were not mathematically precise, thus making it impossible to determine the exact linear equivalent of *uncia,* it has been deemed better, in giving these measurements, to retain the word "cubit" and to translate *uncia* as inch. Thus "inch," as here used, does not equal the twelfth part of a foot, but rather one twenty-fourth of a cubit. And a cubit equals approximately a foot and a half. (Cf. Forcellini, *Lexicon Totius Latinitatis* [6 vols., Patavii: Typis Seminarii, 1940], s. v. *Cubitum,* I, 903; *Uncia,* IV, 858-9.)

The base of the confessional, on which rested the feet of the confessor and the knees of the penitent, was likewise to be of wood, and raised at the most eight inches above the floor of the church. This base was to be two cubits wide and about twice as long. The confessional was to be furnished with a seat which was one cubit three inches high, one and a half cubits wide, and one cubit in depth. The height of the whole confessional was to be four cubits. In the confessor's part there was to be placed a shelf which could be raised or lowered at will and on which the confessor could rest his arm. On the penitent's side a sort of stool to be used as a prie-dieu, fourteen inches wide at the base, leaning against the partition, was to rise obliquely to a height of one cubit twenty inches and to support at the top an inclined table, fourteen inches wide and one and a half cubits long, on which the kneeling penitent could rest his joined hands. The knee-rest, eight inches high and sixteen inches wide, would thus be approximately the same length as the stool.

In the middle of the wooden partition which separated the confessor from the penitent there was to be a small window, the bottom of which began twenty inches above the confessor's seat. The window itself was to be sixteen inches high and twelve inches wide, and divided into three equal parts by two small columns or supports of wood. To this small window was to be fixed, on the penitent's side, a sheet of iron pierced with a large number of small holes about the size of a pea; and, on the confessor's side, it was to be covered with a small piece of light silk or drugget.

Confessionals of this description were to be set up in all churches whether they were cathedral, secular or regular collegiate, parochial, or non-parochial churches. In cathedral churches there were to be constructed as many confessionals as were deemed necessary in accommodation of the great number of penitents desiring to go to confession to gain jubilee indulgences or by reason of some other solemnity. In each one of the secular and regular collegiate churches there was likewise to be a sufficient number of confessionals in proportion to the number of people who were accustomed ordinarily to make their confession there. Parochial churches, according to the "Book of Instructions," were each to have two confessionals, one for men, another for women. The IV Provincial Council, however, allowed a single confessional in small parochial churches where there were less than five hundred souls. In churches where there were more than two priests there were to be as many confessionals as there were confessors. Even in non-parochial churches there were to be two confessionals, whether these churches were by some law subject to a parochial church, joined to it, or set up within its boundaries, or whether the confessor resided at them, or whether the pastor had to or was accustomed to reside at them for any reason whatsoever. If in these non-parochial churches Christian doctrine classes were taught, there was to be at least one confessional; if both sexes received instruction, then there were to be two, or perhaps even more if there were several confessors.

St. Charles even specified the precise location in the church where the confessionals were to be placed. They were to be located on the sides of the church, not too close to the main altar, and in a patent and open place; one on the south side, and one on the north. When the confessor occupied the confessional on the Gospel side of the church, the penitent was to be on his right; and when he used the confessional on the Epistle side, the penitent was to be at his left. In either case the confessor, not the penitent, would thus be closer to the altar, and the penitent would always face the altar. Permission of the bishop was to be obtained if extra confessionals were to be located in other places in the church. For example, confessionals could be placed in chapels if they were amply open to view. St. Charles warned confessors that, while a penitent's confession was being heard, others were not to be allowed to stand close by, since this could endanger the secrecy of the confession.

In each confessional there were to be affixed a crucifix, the letters of the process published every year on Holy Thursday,[53] a list of the cases which the bishop had reserved to himself, the form of absolution, and a printed list of prayers in preparation for the hearing of confessions.[54]

St. Charles forbade confessors to hear confessions in private homes except in cases of infirmity. If, in such cases, the penitent was a woman, the door of the room was to remain open in order that both

53. That is, the list of cases reserved to the Holy See in the Bull *In Coena Domini*, published annually on Maundy Thursday.

54. Cap. V — Mansi, XXXIV A, 227.

confessor and penitent might be seen easily by those who stood at some short distance.[55]

B. HIS INFLUENCE

It is impossible to determine the extent to which these regulations of St. Charles Borromeo may have influenced the practice in other dioceses. It must be remembered that his decrees were merely of a particular nature, binding only in his own province, the province of Milan. Though dioceses outside this province were not obliged to conform to these regulations, some, especially in Italy and France, did in fact follow St. Charles' good example. Thus the Council of Naples (1576)[56] enacted the general law that confessions were to be heard in the confessional. Some dioceses, however, while accepting the basic provisions of these regulations, imposed slightly different models of the confessional, which later became more convenient by custom. Such, for example, were the dioceses of Lombardy in Italy, and of Aix and Toulouse in France.[57]

Their improvement consisted in the introduction of confessionals which admitted the entry not simply of one penitent on one side, but of two penitents on opposite sides, and thus helped to make matters easier for the confessor who would not be compelled to lean always to the same side. This of course did not mean that the confessor tried to hear both penitents at the same time, an abuse which grew up in the Greek Church in the hearing of the confessions of husband and wife, and had to be condemned as such by Pope Benedict XIV (1740-1758) in 1742.[58]

---

55. Borromeo, *Acta*, I, 646.

56. Cap. XVI — Mansi, XXXV B, 821.

57. Villien, *The History and Liturgy of the Sacraments* (English translation by H. W. Edwards, London: Burns, Oates and Washbourne Ltd., 1932), p. 184.

58. Benedictus XIV, const. *Etsi pastoralis*, 26 maii 1742, § V, n. xii — *Bullarii Romani Continuatio Summorum Pontificum* (14 vols., Prati, 1845-1856), I, 202 (hereafter cited *Bullarii Romani Continuatio*); cf. also *Codicis Iuris Canonici Fontes*, cura Emi Petri Card. Gasparri editi (9 vols., Romae [postea Civitate Vaticana]: Typis Polyglottis Vaticanis, 1923-1939). (Vols. VII-IX, ed. cura et studio Emi Iustiniani Card. Serédi), n. 328 (hereafter cited *Fontes*).

Chapter II

THE PERIOD FOLLOWING THE INTRODUCTION OF CONFESSIONALS

Article 1. *Local Conciliar Legislation and Decrees of the Roman Congregations*

A. Sixteenth Century

As seen above, the Council of Naples (1576) was quick to adopt the confessional. It also decreed that priests were not to hear the confessions of either men or women in private homes without a reason to be approved by the ordinary. The word *approbanda,* used in the text of this law, is not to be understood as having imposed an obligation on the ordinary to give his approval once a necessary reason was shown to be present, but rather as asserting that priests could not presume to act even when they considered a necessary cause to be present unless they first secured the approbation of the ordinary. The Council also forbade the confessions of women to be heard even in church before sunrise or after sundown, unless a necessary reason required it, or unless the ordinary for some just reason permitted it. This was the first council to mention explicitly the discretionary powers of the ordinary in permitting deviations from the general rule.

The Provincial Council of Cosenza (1579)[1] introduced a new reason in allowing confessions to be heard outside the confessional. In addition to a reason of necessity, consideration for the person of the penitent could also permit it, as, for example, in the case of a person who enjoyed some position of dignity. Outside these cases, however, confessors who violated the Council's prescriptions were to be punished in a manner deemed justified by the ordinary. In the same year the V Provincial Council of Milan (1579)[2] imposed upon bishops the obligation of seeing that, except in the case of the sick or for some similar urgent reason, confessions, even of men, were heard only in a church or an oratory. Here is found the first mention of oratories as a

1. *De Poenitentia* — Mansi, XXXV, 923.
2. Cap. X — Mansi, XXXIV A, 367-8.

place for the hearing of confessions. Though it is impossible to determine precisely to which type of oratory reference was made, it must have been either a public or a private oratory, for it was not until 1899 that the term "semi-public oratory" was officially adopted by the Sacred Congregation of Rites.[3]

The Provincial Council of Aix in Provence (1585)[4] provided for the introduction of confessionals throughout the province. Parochial churches and also chapels of ease in which confessions were customarily heard were to have at least one confessional. It was to be patterned after the one "which the bishop will take care to have constructed in the cathedral church as soon as possible." The newness of the regulation regarding the confessional is easily seen from the language of this decree. Of course, where there were many souls and many confessors there would also be a proportionate number of confessionals. If the rectors of churches did not within six months conform to the decree of erecting confessionals, they were to be condemned at the discretion of the bishop, and the confessionals were nonetheless to be built and charged to their expense. And if any priest, whether secular or regular, heard the confessions of women outside the confessional, or in a confessional not constructed in the prescribed form or not having a metal screen to separate the confessor from the woman penitent, then the ordinary was to suspend him from the office and ministry of hearing confessions, and even from the exercise of his orders if that seemed advisable to the bishop.

In Mexico the confessional was still unknown when the Mexican Provincial Council was held in 1585. However, the Council required a perforated screen to be used in the hearing of women's confessions.[5] It specifically mentioned that in hospitals and monasteries the confessions of women were not to be heard apart from the use of a confessional seat that was equipped with such a screen. Many other contemporary councils, though they did not prescribe confessionals, since there was as yet no general knowledge of St. Charles Borromeo's new device, nevertheless were careful to give rules of prudence in their

3. S. R. C., decr. 23 ian. 1899 — *Fontes*, n. 6288.
4. *Quae ad Sacramentum poenitentiae pertinent* — Mansi, XXXIV B, 954.
5. § VI — Mansi, XXXIV B, 1168.

statutes concerning the place for the hearing of confessions. Quite generally it was required that priests hear confessions in an open and not obscure place in the church, and not in the sacristy nor in the room of a private home. In the church there was to be a seat for the confessor and a table with a perforated partition, ordinarily made of metal, dividing him from the penitent. Outside such a place he was not to hear confessions, least of all those of women, no matter of what age or of what class they might be, unless it was a case of necessity or of illness. And in some cases these regulations were strengthened through the threat of penalties to be imposed by the bishop.[6]

The Council of Trani (1589)[7] spoke of *confessoriola,* a term evidently synonymous with *confessionalia,* and required that they be placed in each church, but not in the chapels, that is, the chapels within the church. The reason for this was that such chapels were not always entirely open to view.

By the last decade of the sixteenth century, confessionals were in use in the ecclesiastical provinces of Aix, Toulouse, Sorrento, Salerno, Benevento, Fermo, Sienna, and of course Milan, just to mention a few. And the councils held in these provinces firmly insisted that the confessions of women were not to be heard outside the confessional. The Council of Toulouse (1590)[8] permitted an exception only in cases of sickness and of most grave and imminent danger, and the Council of Sienna (1599)[9] inflicted an *ipso facto* incurred suspension on confessors who violated its prescription. However, in some cases, as for example in the province of Rheims, though the confessional was adopted, its use was not prescribed in a positive and rigorous manner in the

6. Cf. Council of Manfredonia (1567), *De Poenitentia* — Mansi, XXXV B, 879; Council of Ravenna (1568), Cap. II — Mansi, XXXV A, 619-20; Council of Urbino (1569), Cap. II — Mansi, XXXV A, 664; Council of Capua (1569), *De Sacramento Poenitentiae* — Mansi, XXXV A, 712; Council of Besançon (1571), Mansi, XXXVI bis, 54; Council of Florence (1573), Cap. III — Mansi, XXXV A, 762; Council of Genoa (1574), Cap. X — Mansi, XXXVI bis, 574; Council of Bordeaux (1583), Cap. XII — Mansi, XXXIV A, 758; Council of Bourges (1584), Can. XVIII — Mansi, XXXIV A, 902.

7. *De Sacramento Poenitentiae,* n. 2 — Mansi, XXXVI bis, 875.

8. Cap. IV, n. 10 — Mansi, XXXIV B, 1286.

9. Cap. VI, n. 5 — Mansi, XXXVI bis, 532.

dioceses which composed the province. In fact, according to several even later Rituals as used by these dioceses, confessors seemed to enjoy a certain freedom in this regard.[10]

The first decree to be issued by any of the Roman Sacred Congregations in regard to the confessional as such seems to have come from the Sacred Congregation of Bishops and Regulars on September 22, 1592.[11] In this case, among several suggestions which it made to the Bishop of Vicenza concerning an institute of St. Peter, the Sacred Congregation mentioned that the confessional for the nuns was to be located in church. The following year this same Congregation stated that in general it was most fitting that confessors hear confessions in church, except when the penitent suffered from infirmity or when some other similar fitting reason warranted the hearing of the confession outside the church.[12]

A decree under date of May, 1596, in referring to the canon penitentiary, said that he was to hear confessions in the confessional unless the penitent should desire to confess in some other fitting place in the church. It remained for the bishop, however, in such a case to grant permission to the penitentiary to yield to the will of the penitent.[13]

The Council of Salerno (1596),[14] besides decreeing that *confessionaria* be set up in every parochial church, legislated that confessions were always to be heard only in them and in designated places, except on the vigil of Christmas. Here, apparently, was implicitly contained the introduction of a new reason for hearing confessions outside the

10. Barraud, "Notice sur les Confessionaux," *Bulletin Monumental* (Paris: 1834-1896), XXXIV (1868), 831.

11. S. C. Ep. et Reg., *Vicentina,* 22 sept. 1592 — *Fontes,* n. 1464.

12. S. C. Ep. et Reg., *in Neapolitana,* 29 mart. 1593, as cited by Ferraris, *Prompta Bibliotheca Canonica, Iuridica, Moralis, Theologica, necnon Ascetica, Polemica, Rubricistica, Historica* (9 vols., Romae: 1885-1899), s. v. *Confessarius,* art. III, n. 7 (hereafter cited *Prompta Bibliotheca*).

13. Cited by Pallottini, *Collectio Omnium Conclusionum et Resolutionum quae in causis propositis apud Sacram Congregationem Cardinalium S. Concilii Tridentini Interpretum prodierunt ab eius institutione anno MDLXIV ad annum MDCCCLX, distinctis titulis alphabetico ordine per materias digesta* (17 vols., Romae: 1868-1893), s. v. *Sacramentum Poenitentiae,* n. 24 (hereafter cited *Collectio*).

14. Cap. XIII — Mansi, XXXV B, 987.

ordinary place, namely, the great number of penitents. For it can easily be imagined, as judged from the present practice, how large must have been the number of faithful who approached this holy sacrament in preparation for the feast of Christmas.

B. SEVENTEENTH CENTURY

In the diocese of Malines in Belgium the confessional had already been introduced by the year 1607. The Provincial Council of Malines (1607) decreed that wherever confessionals had not yet been constructed they were to be erected within three months from the date of the publication of the Council's decrees. And from that time onward anyone who presumed without the permission of the ordinary to hear the confessions of women outside the confessional, except in cases of necessity, was to be punished.[15] This Council clearly indicated the existence of a second compartment in the confessional to be used by the penitent. In his *Commentary* on the Roman Ritual, Catalani (+ after 1751) called this the *sedes bimestris*.[16] Later on, for reasons of convenience, still another compartment was introduced, thus making a tri-partite confessional.

According to a declaration made by Abbé Straub, professor of archaeology in the seminary of Strasbourg, at the archaeological congress held in that city in 1856, confessionals in France do not date back further than the seventeenth century.[17] But, as has already been seen from a decree of the Council of Aix in Provence (1585), the confessional was certainly known there before the seventeenth century. However, if Abbé Straub's statement is interpreted to mean that a widespread use of the confessional was not known until the seventeenth century, then it appears that he is correct. Furthermore, another scholarly archaeologist, the Norman Abbé Cochet, in a letter dated June 1, 1869, supported this opinion. He wrote:

15. Tit. V, Cap. III — Mansi, XXXIV B, 1448.

16. *Rituale Romanum Benedicti Papae XIV iussu editum cum Commentariis Catalani* (Patavii, 1760), tit. III, ch. I, n. 8, p. 197, as cited by Barraud, "Notice sur les Confessionaux," *Bulletin Monumental,* XXXIV (1868), 839.

17. Quoted by Cochet, "Lettre sur les confessionaux au moyen-age," *Bulletin Monumental,* XXXVII (1871), 52. (Note: The author is thus identified in Villien, p. 180).

> I have visited all the churches of the diocese of Rouen, and I do not think I have ever come across a confessional of the time of Louis XIII. I saw many of the eighteenth century, but those of the seventeenth century are extremely rare, even if any at all are to be found. I remember having met with one in a country church in the neighborhood of Bernay: but this was in the diocese of Evreux. . . . This state of affairs is almost general throughout France.[18]

The Provincial Council of Narbonne (1609)[19] enacted a statute which required every church to have confessionals located in an open place in the church.

On June 17, 1614, Paul V (1605-1621) with his Constitution *Apostolicae Sedis* authorized the publication of the first edition of the official Roman Ritual. The Ritual stated that priests were to hear confessions in church, and not in private homes, except for a good reason. In all cases they were to employ a fitting place which was open to full view. The confessional, located in an apt place in the church, was to be provided with a perforated screen. These prescriptions remained unchanged until the typical edition of 1925, in which the wording of the Code of Canon Law was adopted.[20]

The Sacred Congregation of Bishops and Regulars on September 16, 1617, approved the statute of a certain ordinary in which he forbade regulars to hear in their cells the confessions of outsiders. Three years later this same Sacred Congregation ordered the confessions of women not to be heard before sunrise or after sunset unless necessary.[21]

The Diocesan Synod of Rouen (1618) decided that, for the convenience of confessors and penitents alike, there should be confessionals in all the churches.[22] The Council of Bordeaux (1624)[23] decreed that confessionals be located in all the churches in an open place, and not in any of the chapels, in any corners of the church, or in the sacristy.

---

18. Translation as given in Villien, p. 180.
19. Cap. XVI — Mansi, XXXIV B, 1494.
20. *Rituale Rom. Pauli V Pont. Max. Iussu Editum* (Romae: Typis Sac. Cong. de Prop. Fide, 1658), p. 81.
21. Both decrees cited in Ferraris, *Prompta Bibliotheca*, s. v. *Confessarius*, art. III, n. 8.
22. Cochet, "Lettre sur les confessionaux au moyen age," *Bulletin Monumental*, XXXVII (1871), 51.
23. Cap. V — Can. 11, Mansi, XXXIV B, 1554.

It also provided that in the cathedral church a priest-penitentiary was within three months to be appointed by the bishop for the hearing of confessions at stated hours during the day in a confessional situated in an open and patent place. If he was a canon, he was to be considered as being present at choir the while he actually heard confessions in the church; not so, however, if he heard them outside the church, even though the penitent was sick.[24]

Maschat (1692-1747) referred to a decree of the Sacred Congregation of Bishops and Regulars under date of July 10, 1625, which stated that confessions were to be heard in a church in a confessional equipped with a screen, but that they might be heard also in a case of necessity or for some good reason even in the sacristy or in some other fitting place. The Sacred Congregation also stated that bishops could not, in person or through their delegates, visit the confessionals or places of regulars where confessions were heard, not even to see if their own decrees had been carried out. This was to be left absolutely to the visitation of the regulars' own superiors.[25]

The Provincial Council of Cambrai (1631)[26] decreed that within four months after the publication of its statutes confessionals were to be erected in all the churches. It added that no one was to presume without the permission of the ordinary to hear the confessions of women outside these confessionals, except in a case of necessity. The fact that it recognized explicitly the ordinary's right and duty of vigilance is important, for in this way could abuses all the more easily be forestalled. The obligation, however, of having a properly equipped confessional in church devolved upon the pastor.[27]

The "Ritual of Beauvais" (1637) stated that the priest was to hear confessions in a patent, conspicuous and apt place in church, and not in the corners of chapels or in the sanctuary. Where conveniently

---

24. Barbosa, *Pastoralis Solicitudinis sive de Officio et Potestate Episcopi Tripartita Descriptio* (Lugduni, 1628), Pars III, p. 107, n. 30 (hereafter cited *De Officio Episcopi*).

25. Maschat, *Institutiones Canonicae* (4 vols. in 2, Florentiae, 1854), II, Pars I, 86.

26. Tit. X, Cann. 4-5 — Mansi, XXXVI ter, 175.

27. Barbosa, *Pastoralis Solicitudinis sive de Officio et Potestate Parochi Tripartita Descriptio* (Lugduni, 1655), Pars II, p. 158, n. 59.

possible, some barrier was to be placed between the confessor and the penitent. The priest was to be seated as a judge; he was not to remain standing or kneeling, nor was he to lean on the altar. He was not to hear confessions in homes except for a grave reason, in which case there was always postulated a fitting and open place. At night the place was to be well-lighted, especially when the penitent was a woman.[28]

The Sacred Congregation of Bishops and Regulars on September 22, 1645, issued a decree commanding all confessors, whether secular or regular, when hearing the confessions of any lay persons, no matter of what age or sex, to hear them in a church and in a confessional equipped with a screen having perforations about the size of the tip of one's little finger. But in cases of necessity or infirmity, it allowed confessions to be heard in the sacristy or in some other fitting place, or at home, even without the pastor's permission, provided, however, that a written note was left in testimony of the fact of the confession, or that the pastor was notified in person concerning the same.[29]

In 1660 the Sacred Congregation for the Propagation of the Faith, in a decree to the Archbishop of Sofia, made the use of the confessional compulsory. It enjoined him to build permanent and immovable confessionals in all the larger churches. In the smaller churches there was no obligation to erect a confessional. However, in such cases, whether confessions were heard in the church or perhaps outside, because of the large number of people, it was absolutely forbidden, under threat of heavy penalties, to hear them without an immovable table equipped with a small screen between the confessor and the penitent, especially in the case of women.[30]

It was only in 1693 that confessionals were introduced in the diocese of Avranches, and seven years later in Lisieux.[31]

---

28. *Manuale Bellovacense Reverendi in Christo Domini D. Augustini Potier Episcopi et Comitis Bellovacensis ac Franciae paris auctoritate restitutum* (Bellovaci, 1637), pp. 76-77 as cited by Barraud, "Notice sur les Confessionaux," *Bulletin Monumental*, XXXIV (1868), 831.

29. S. C. Ep. et Reg., *Pisauren.*, 22 sept. 1645 — *Fontes*, n. 1774.

30. S. C. de Prop. Fide (C. G.), 22 febr. 1660 — *Fontes*, n. 4464.

31. Cochet, "Lettre sur les confessionaux au moyen age," *Bulletin Monumental*, XXXVII (1871), 52.

The Provincial Council of Naples (1699),[32] in declaring that confessions were to be heard in church except in cases of necessity, allowed an exception to be made in the case of priests who could not easily go to confession in church. For the violation of the conciliar prescription the offending priest was disqualified from hearing confessions and could also be punished in other ways. If, in hearing the confessions of women, a confessor, whether secular, regular, or exempt in any way, did not use a confessional, or used one which did not meet the necessary requirements, he was to be suspended from the hearing of confessions. For example, the penalty could take effect if the perforations in the confessional screen were too large. The Council also suspended from the hearing of confessions any confessor who, in hearing the confession of a sick woman, did not leave the door of the room open, so that both he and the penitent could be seen.

Pignatelli (+ after 1700) mentioned that for an urgent reason the sacrament of penance could be administered even in private homes to laymen and to priests who could not go to church because of old age or infirmity. In such cases neither diocesan synodal constitutions nor any other ordinances could effectively set up any prohibition to the contrary.[33]

C. EIGHTEENTH CENTURY

After considering the statutes of the Diocesan Synod of Cagli (1711-1717), the Sacred Congregation of Bishops and Regulars in 1719 asked the Bishop of Cagli to abolish the suspension *a divinis* incurred *ipso facto* by those confessors who heard confessions outside the church, except when warranted to do so in a case of infirmity, and by those who, while hearing the confessions of women in church, nevertheless heard them outside the confessional seat. The Sacred Congregation thought that suspension from the hearing of confessions was quite sufficient as a canonical penalty.[34]

---

32. Cann. 10-11 — Mansi, XXXVI ter, 746.

33. *Consultationes Canonicae* (11 vols. in 5, Coloniae Allobrogum, 1700), X, 56, n. 43; cf. also Pallottini, *Collectio*, s. v. *Sacramentum Poenitentiae* n. 116).

34. Bizzarri, *Collectanea*, p. 341.

On November 28, 1725, the Sacred Congregation of the Holy Office issued a decree concerning the Vicariate Apostolic of Tunkin. The Sacred Congregation for the Propagation of the Faith had sent to the Holy Office for consideration a copy of a decree introduced by the Bishop of the Vicariate, which commanded that a reed-screen with small perforations be used in the hearing of women's confessions. If such a screen was not used, the woman penitent could not be considered absolved, and the confessor was deemed to have committed a sacrilege, for in such a case his faculties to absolve were withdrawn, unless, of course, the woman was ill. The Holy Office ordered that the whole decree be amended so that priests were forbidden simply to hear the confessions of women without such a screen when it could conveniently be had, mention of all penalties being omitted, especially that which affected the validity of the confession.[35]

From these two decrees it is easily seen that the Sacred Congregations, while desiring that the proper precautions be taken in the hearing of women's confessions, nevertheless did not intend the regulations to be so rigid as to allow an exception only in a case of illness. Nor was it desirable that severe penalties be imposed, least of all one that could affect the validity of the absolution.

The Provincial Council of Avignon (1725)[36] contained a statute which strongly cautioned confessors against hearing confessions outside the confessional, especially those of women and girls, unless there was question of a serious illness. Exception could also be made when, because of the large number desiring to go to confession or because of the lack of a sufficient number of confessionals, the faithful would otherwise be deprived of the opportunity of receiving this sacrament. In such circumstances, however, the confessor had to choose at least a patent place and use the sleeve of his surplice or some other linen cloth, such as a handkerchief, to shield his face.

The Council of Mt. Lebanon (1736)[37] legislated that each church should have a confessional seat, equipped with a perforated screen, located in a conspicuous but fitting place in the church. Confessions

---

35. S. C. S. Off., 28 nov. 1725, ad 8 — *Fontes,* n. 785.
36. Cap. III — Mansi, XXXVII, 324-5.
37. Pars II, Cap. IV, Can. 10 — Mansi, XXXVIII, 55.

were to be heard there and not in private homes, except for some good reason, in which case, however, they were still to be heard in a fitting and open place. Any priest, whether secular or regular, even if a pastor, who violated this prescription was to be punished according to the discretion of the ordinary, unless the penitent had been a priest who could not conveniently go to confession in church.

Pope Benedict XIV, in his Encyclical Letter *Magno cum* under date of June 2, 1751, recalled the norms established by the Roman Ritual in regard to the hearing of confessions: *In ecclesia, non autem in privatis aedibus, confessiones [sacerdos] audiat, nisi ex causa rationabili, quae cum inciderit, studeat tamen id decenti, ac patenti loco praestare.*[38] He also repeated very approvingly St. Charles Borromeo's exhortation to the superiors of regulars to see that these prescriptions were carried out exactly. It seems that regulars had, by basing their claim on the bull *Superna* of Pope Clement X (1670-1676),[39] asserted for themselves the faculty of hearing the confessions of the faithful with no limitation as regards place. But Benedict XIV did not, outside the cases admitted in the law, recognize the privilege of regulars to hear confessions in private homes: *Nullam facultatem esse tributam Regularibus audiendi confessiones sacramentales in privatis domibus, ac proinde minime licere eisdem Regularibus cuiusvis Ordinis . . . Sacramentum Poenitentiae administrare in domibus privatis extra casus iure permissos.*[40]

The Sacred Congregation for the Propagation of the Faith on June 12, 1764, when asked whether the Bishop Visitator of Tunkin rightfully required the confessions of women not to be heard without a screen interposed between the confessor and the penitent, except in a case of necessity, answered in the affirmative, adding: *iuxta ordines pluries datos a S. C.*[41]

The "Ritual of Senlis" (1764) hardly differed from that of Augustine Potier in the rules it set down for the hearing of confessions.

38. Benedictus XIV, ep. encycl. *Magno cum,* 2 iun. 1751, § 20 — *Fontes,* n. 413.

39. Clemens X, *Superna,* 21 iun. 1670 — *Fontes,* n. 246.

40. Benedictus XIV, ep. encycl. *Magno cum,* 2 iun. 1751, § 20 — *Fontes,* n. 413.

41. S. C. de Prop. Fide (C. P. pro Sin.-Tunkin), 12 iun. 1764 — *Fontes,* n. 4542.

It considered it sufficient to exact the use of a confessional as long as this could be done conveniently: *Ubi commode fieri poterit.*[42]

The Sacred Congregation for the Propagation of the Faith in 1780 found it necessary to remind regulars of the penal sanctions enacted against allowing women to enter their cloister. It had been brought to the Sacred Congregation's attention that, in stations and hospitals of missionaries, women had sometimes been admitted, and their confessions heard in rooms or in other places in the hospital. The Congregation strongly reproved this practice:

> Quod quidem quam indecorum sit, quamque periculosum, probe noscens Sacra Congregatio, quae missionarios suos inter christiani nominis hostes versantes, non solum a malo, sed etiam ab omni specie mali abstinere desiderat, ut, iuxta Apostoli monitum, sine offensione sint iudaeis, et gentibus, et Ecclesiae Dei; . . . statuit ac iussit hospitia et stationes, seu domus quaslibet cuiuscumque Ordinis, Congregationis, aut instituti Regularis, in locis Missionum ubicumque existentes, in quibus duo vel tres missionarii latini ritus commorantur, seu commorari contigerit, clausurae legibus subiici, ita ut nemini regulari cuicumque omnino liceat, ullam foeminam intra privata eorumdem hospitiorum seu stationum cubicula, mansiones, recessus, sub quovis titulo, specie, ac praetextu introducere, multoque minus sanctissimum Poenitentiae Sacramentum ibidem ipsis administrare; . . . Ut autem ad eorumdem hospitiorum interna oratoria, ecclesias, ac loca, ubi sacra peraguntur, mulieribus quoque pateat accessus, ut sacrosanctae Missae Sacrificio, aliisque ecclesiasticis functionibus, intersint, atque Sacramentum Poenitentiae suscipiant; . . . iubet praeterea et praecipit Sacra Congregatio, ut mulierum confessiones palam in ecclesiis, cappellis, aut publicis oratoriis, ubi adsunt: ubi vero desiderantur, in alio loco patenti, ac pervio, et ianuae hospitii quantum fieri potest viciniori, a respectivis Ordinariis, et his deficientibus, a localibus Missionum Superioribus designando, interposita crate ferrea, vel alio repagulo inter os confessarii, ac mulieris poenitentis, audiantur. Qui secus fecerint, ac saluberrimis hisce ordinationibus contraiverint, poenas contra clausurae violatores, ac sacrorum canonum, et Apostolicarum Constitutionum praefatarum contemptores incurrant. . . . Sanctitas Sua be-

---

42. *Rituale ad usum dioecesis Silvanectensis, auctoritate illustrissimi ac reverendissimi D. Ioannis Armandi de Roquelaure episcopi Silvanectensis editum* (Silvanecti, 1764), *Ordo administrandi Sacr. Poen.*, p. 150, as cited by Barraud, "Notice sur Les Confessionaux," *Bulletin Monumental,* XXXIV (1868), 833.

nigne [hoc] confirmavit, Apostolicae Suae auctoritatis robur adiiciens, et ab omnibus sub memoratis poenis inviolabiliter observari iussit.[43]

The Diocesan Synod of Ferrara (1781) with reference to the hearing of confessions gave rules which clearly indicated how crystallized such regulations had become. Confessionals were to be equipped with a minutely perforated screen and set up in a conspicuous, open and well-lighted place in the church. The sacrament was to be administered there, and never in homes, except for a fitting and just reason. The confessions of women were to be heard only in the confessional in the church, never in sacristies or homes, except in cases of the penitent's infirmity. Their confessions were not to be heard before daybreak or after the evening *Angelus,* except for a similar reason. To violate even a part of these prescriptions resulted in the deprivation of the faculties for the hearing of confessions. If necessity required that the sacrament be administered at home, the door of the room was to be left open, so that the confessor and penitent could be seen. Moreover, he was to shield his face from the penitent's view by raising his hand or by using a handkerchief. This was to be done even in the case of men whenever their confession was heard outside the confessional.[44]

On March 17, 1785, the Sacred Congregation for the Propagation of the Faith decreed that in the mission of Chan-si in China the use of the confessional grille was obligatory. But if it became impossible to observe this ruling when confessions were out of necessity heard in a private home, then it was sufficient for women-penitents to cover their face with a veil.[45]

Perhaps, despite the great and varying detail regarding the place for the hearing of confessions, all could be summed up with laconic simplicity as did Pilatus (1705-1755) in these words: *Locus administrandae poenitentiae consuetus ecclesia est, nisi iusta causa aliter suaserit. Tunc omnis aptus est locus.*[46]

---

43. S. C. de Prop. Fide, decr. 26 aug. 1780 — *Fontes,* n. 4582.
44. *Synodus Dioecesana Ferrariensis* (Ferrariae, 1781), p. 96.
45. S. C. de Prop. Fide (C. P. pro Sin. — Chan-si), 17 mart. 1785 — *Fontes,* n. 4600.
46. *Origines Iuris Pontificii ad Carolum Sextum* (Tridenti, 1739), p. 218.

D. NINETEENTH CENTURY

The Provincial Council of Szechuan in China (1803) enacted comparatively lengthy regulations to be followed in the hearing of confessions. The place was to be patent, fitting, beyond all suspicion, and easily visible to all. No mention, however, was made regarding the hearing of confessions in church. That, no doubt, was due to the fact that, because of the missionary character of the vicariate, there existed the custom of hearing confessions in private homes or in the confessor's room. That also accounts for the fact that the Council omitted all mention of confessionals as such. Nevertheless, it stressed the importance of having a screen to divide the confessor from the penitent, and ordered that the door of the room be always left open. Since the use of such a screen reflected not only a customary usage but also a prescription of the Church, and since it was relatively easy to procure one, no confessor was to be without one. In fact, the Council stated that he could easily carry it with him.

Since this Council, mindful of the difficulties encountered because of missionary-country circumstances, adapted its regulations accordingly, its prescriptions seem important enough to quote:

> Praeterea maturo et diuturno examine adhibito, circumstantiisque rerum serio perpensis, cum in hac regione nihil prorsus nunc impediat vel obstet, quominus confessiones excipiantur interposita crate iuxta praescriptum et consuetudinem Ecclesiae, immo gravissimae causae rationesque saluberrimam hanc regulam servandam suadeant, hinc de consilio Illmi. Petri Caradrensis Episcopi, coadiutoris nostri, statuimus ac praecipimus omnibus et singulis missionariis huius vicariatus, sive europaeis sive indigenis, ut in qualibet christianitate confessiones excipiant, praeterquam infirmorum, interposita crate lignea vel arundinea (quae quidem ubique facile confici potest, ad instar fenestrae pedibus ligneis superpositae, ut sunt ea tabulata perforata ante aulae ianuam posita . . .) aut interposito velamento ex virgis arundineis et raris . . . (quod facile secum deferri potest et suspendi inter sacerdotem et poenitentem). Praedicta autem crates et velamentum habeant saltem duos pedes longitudinis et duos latitudinis: his cautionibus adhibitis fiet, ut nemini detur offensio, nec oblocutionibus vel suspicionibus locus, plurimaque praecaveantur pericula tum pro sacerdote, tum pro poenitente, eo quidem maiora, quod in aedibus fidelium saepe nullus alius re-

periatur locus ad excipiendas confessiones idoneus, praeter sacerdotis cubiculum.[47]

The Sacred Congregation for the Propagation of the Faith issued a decree on April 13, 1807, which stated that it was not permissible for priests of the Chaldean rite to hear the confessions of the faithful in private homes, unless there was some reasonable excuse. When such an excuse was verified, especially in the hearing of women's confessions, the door of the room was to be left open so that both the confessor and the penitent could be seen.[48]

In 1821 this same Congregation was asked if it was required to take any precautions when it was necessary to hear, without an interposed screen, the confessions of women in private homes. The reply stated that it was to be left to the discretion of the bishop, who was to weigh well the justness of the reason. Once he had given the faculty of hearing the confessions of women in private homes, he should enjoin upon confessors the obligation never to hear the confessions of women without a screen or some other such barrier, except in the case of those confined to their beds. But in this case the door of the room was to remain ajar, so that both the confessor and the penitent remained within possible ready observation.[49]

The I Provincial Council of Baltimore (1829) in its twenty-fifth decree strongly exhorted the erection of confessionals in all the public churches of the province, which then included most of the territory which now constitutes the United States. Once such confessionals were set up, no priest was to be permitted to hear the confessions of women in any other place without the special permission of the ordinary. This permission, the Council hoped, would never be granted except to confessors who were of an advanced age or infirm, or if the penitent was hard of hearing, or in other cases in which the observance of the regulation entailed grave inconvenience. But even in such cases the confessions were never to be heard in private homes unless some kind of screen was interposed between the confessor and the penitent, and un-

47. Cap. VI, can. 13 — Mansi, XXXIX, 34.

48. S. C. de Prop. Fide, decr. 13 apr. 1807, n. xiii — *Fontes,* n. 4691.

49. S. C. de Prop. Fide (C. G. — Hiberniae), 12 febr. 1821 — *Fontes,* n. 4723.

less the place was open, at least as much as the particular circumstances allowed.[50]

This decree originally forbade all confessions to be heard privately, but the Sacred Congregation for the Propagation of the Faith limited its application to the confessions of women and girls. It also thought the provision should be added that, when the confessions of women were heard outside the confessional in consequence of the special permission of the ordinary, this should be done in a patent place, as far as it was possible, and never without a *crates*.[51]

Pope Gregory XVI (1831-1846) in an apostolic letter under date of February 3, 1832, complained to the Armenian Archbishop Primate at Constantinople of the practice of frequently hearing confessions in private homes. In order to prevent all the abuses which might easily arise from such a custom, the Holy Father urged the Archbishop to examine the situation very thoroughly. He also cautioned against granting such a permission to all priests indiscriminately. Rather, it was to be given only to those priests whose deep piety placed them above all suspicion. Even then it was to be granted only for the benefit of morally upright laymen who had an apt place set apart for such a purpose, one not put to profane uses, and one in which the sacrament could be administered without danger of profanation.[52]

On September 21, 1840, the Sacred Congregation for the Propagation of the Faith gave a response stating that where there were churches and public oratories it was forbidden to hear women's confessions in homes, except for reasons of infirmity, advanced age or deafness.[53]

The V Provincial Council of Baltimore (1843) repeated the I Provincial Council's decree concerning the construction of confessionals in churches, and commanded that it be strictly observed. It added that by the word "church" was not to be understood the sacristy, unless it was a public and patent place.[54]

---

50. Decr. XXV — *Acta et Decreta Sacrorum Conciliorum Recentiorum, Collectio Lacensis* (7 vols., Friburgi Brisgoviae, 1870-1892), III, 30-31 (hereafter cited *Collectio Lacensis*).

51. *Collectio Lacensis*, III, 24; Decr. XXV — *Collectio Lacensis*, III, 30-31.

52. Gregorius XVI, ep. encycl. *Inter gravissimas*, 3 febr. 1832 — *Fontes*, n. 483.

53. S. C. de Prop. Fide (C. G.), 21 sept. 1840, ad 8 — *Fontes*, n. 4784.

54. Decr. IX — *Collectio Lacensis*, III, 90.

The I Provincial Council of Australia, held at Sydney (1844), stated that sacramental confessions should always be heard in a church or a chapel, if possible. Priests, however, could go to confession in any convenient place, and those who were deaf could be heard in any place.[55] In a Plenary Council, also held at Sydney (1885), it was decreed that in all churches there should be a confessional seat equipped with a screen. Pastors were exhorted to hear confessions in church as much as possible, and never to hear them anywhere but in a decent place with the doors open. Except in cases of necessity, women's confessions were to be heard only in the confessional seat in church.[56]

The Diocesan Synod of Fermo (1845) prescribed that confessions be heard in a confessional seat in the church. However, it permitted men who were more than eighteen years of age to be heard in the sacristy. It was never permissible to hear the confessions of women outside the confessional seat, or even in it face to face. In private homes confessions could be heard only in cases of necessity, infirmity, or for some other good reason to be approved by the ordinary. The Synod added that regulars were allowed to hear in their monasteries the confessions of men.[57]

Neither the sacristy nor any place other than the confessional seat located in the church was to be used for the hearing of women's confessions, according to the Provincial Council of Rouen (1850). If however it was necessary to use the sacristy to hear the confession of a woman because of deafness or in consequence of any other infirmity which might require it, the confessor was still to use some sort of table with a perforated screen.[58]

The Council of Toulouse (1850) inflicted an *ipso facto* contracted suspension on confessors who outside the cases of necessity heard the confessions of women in a place other than a sacred and public one, or who did not use a screen. By way of example it mentioned as a legitimate excusing reason the sickness or deafness of the penitent.[59]

---

55. Decr. XII, *De Sacramento Poenitentiae — Collectio Lacensis,* III, 1051.
56. Cann. 130-131 — *Acta et Decreta Concilii Plenarii Australasiae Primi, anno 1885* (Sydney, 1887), p. 42.
57. Decr. XIII — *Dioecesana Synodus Firmana* (Firmi, 1845), p. 121.
58. Decr. XVII, n. 3 — *Collectio Lacensis,* IV, 530.
59. Tit. III, Cap. I, Decr. LXX — *Collectio Lacensis,* IV, 1054.

The Council of Cashel (1853) stated that, although it was especially desirable that the confessions of the faithful always be heard in church, nevertheless the circumstances in that province were such that the custom of having "confessional stations" in the homes of the faithful could not be absolutely abolished without great harm to religion.[60] The II Council of Tuam (1854) permitted them in public places where the people could not easily reach the church. As places for the hearing of confessions, their use was forbidden in private homes, in cities or towns having churches, and in all places which were not too distant from a church. When they were used, the pastor was to see to it that confessions were heard in a patent and decent place.[61]

The I Provincial Council of Westminster, England (1852), required confessionals to be erected in churches in which they had not yet been constructed. But if locally some special difficulty was involved, then the matter was to be left to the judgment of the ordinary. The usual provision concerning women's confessions was also included in its decrees.[62]

The II Provincial Council of Quebec (1854), in addition to repeating the prescription of the Roman Ritual, added a particular regulation because of the especially cold climate in that region. Thus, in summer the confessional seat was to be located in the church, but in winter it could be placed in the sacristy.[63]

That same year the Council of Port of Spain (1854) was held, with the colonies of England, Holland, and Denmark in the West Indies taking part. It was decreed that in all public churches, especially parochial churches, confessionals were to be erected. Except for a good reason it was there, or at least in a sacred oratory, that confessions were to be heard. Women were never to be heard at home without the ordinary's permission, except in a case of illness. Even then, however, a confessional screen was to be used.[64]

---

60. *De Poenitentia* — *Collectio Lacensis,* III, 837.

61. Decr. VIII — *Collectio Lacensis,* III, 860; cf. also Council of Thurles (1850), Decr. XIV, nn. 40-41, 48 — *Collectio Lacensis,* III, 782; Provincial Council of Dublin (1853), Decr. XVII — *Collectio Lacensis,* III, 807; Provincial Council of Armagh (1854), Decr. XII — *Collectio Lacensis,* III, 850.

62. Decr. XIX, n. 1 — *Collectio Lacensis,* III, 934.

63. Decr. IX, § 7, n. 2 — *Collectio Lacensis,* III, 639.

64. Art. IV, nn. 1-2 — *Collectio Lacensis,* III, 1098.

The Council of Ravenna (1855) noted that, since confessions were to be heard publicly and openly in the churches, confessionals were to be placed in the churches in an open and public place. Then it proceeded to describe how such confessionals were to be constructed, that is, with a minutely perforated metal screen separating the confessor from the penitent. Women and children who had not reached the age of puberty were never to be heard in private homes. As a matter of fact, the confessions of women were never to be heard except in the confessional. Any priest delinquent in regard to this regulation was *ipso facto* suspended from the hearing of confessions. The usual exception, of course, was to be made for the infirm. However, if the woman was not confined to her bed, the confessor was expected to request the bishop's permission to hear her confession.

This same Council admonished physicians of their duty, when called to the bedside of a patient in actual danger of death, or even outside such danger whenever the doctor prudently judged that the illness might become dangerous, to see that the patient received the sacrament of penance. Moreover, the physician was not to visit the patient again, if, after three days, the confessor had not been called. This regulation was enforceable by means of canonical penalties to be imposed at the discretion of the bishop.[65]

The I Provincial Council of Halifax (1857) prescribed as a general rule that confessional seats equipped with screens be located in all the churches, and left the matter to the bishop's judgment whenever there was question of such places wherein this regulation could not be strictly carried out.[66]

The Provincial Council of Vienna (1858) decreed that the confessions of women were not to be heard except in a confessional seat located either in the church or in the sacristy.[67] The Council of Cologne (1860), on the other hand, prescribed that the confessions of women be heard only in the confessional in church, and never in the sacristy or

---

65. Decr. IV-V — *Collectio Lacensis*, VI, 159; Decr. XII — *Collectio Lacensis*, VI, 161; cf. also Council of Rome (1725), Tit. XXII, Cap. I — *Collectio Lacensis*, I, 392-393; Council of Bordeaux (1583), Cap. XII — Mansi, XXXIV A, 758.

66. Decr. XIV, n. 1 — *Collectio Lacensis*, III, 745.

67. Cap. VII — *Collectio Lacensis*, V, 169.

in private homes, except in cases wherein the penitent was hard of hearing, advanced in years, or infirm. In such circumstances, however, it was strongly forbidden to hear their confessions without leaving the door of the room ajar.[68]

In regard to hearing at night in parochial churches the confessions, not only of women, but even of men, the Sacred Congregation for the Propagation of the Faith in 1858 wrote to Archbishop John Purcell of Cincinnati that the practice could be tolerated temporarily. Nevertheless, vigilance was to be exercised for the prevention of abuses and for the forestalling of all occasions of scandal.[69]

The V Council of Prague (1860) made the rule that for the hearing of confessions a confessional located in the church was ordinarily to be used. In sacristies, however, especially the larger ones, a confessional equipped with the proper screen could be placed for the convenience of those who were hard of hearing, aged, or infirm. It was forbidden, except in a case of necessity, to hear the confessions of women anywhere but in a church in a properly constructed confessional. Any violation of these prescriptions was to be considered as an intolerable abuse, and the delinquent priest was to be suspended from his office as confessor.[70]

Since the decrees of the II Plenary Council of Baltimore (1866) bound the whole United States, they were of great importance. Nevertheless its legislation did not differ from that of the I Provincial Council of Baltimore (1829), whose decrees have already been considered.[71]

The Provincial Council of Utrecht (1865), in repeating the substantial elements of the many decrees already cited, spoke of places "designated" for the hearing of confessions. It said in part: *Excepto infirmitatis casu, vel nisi alia rationabilis causa adsit, sacramentum poe-*

---

68. Cap. XIV — *Collectio Lacensis*, V, 351.

69. *Collectio Lacensis*, III, 213.

70. Cap. VIII — *Collectio Lacensis*, V, 508; Cap. VIII — *Collectio Lacensis*, V, 543.

71. Tit. V, Cap. V, nn. 295-296 — *Concilii Plenarii Baltimorensis II in Ecclesia Metropolitana Baltimorensi a die VII ad diem XXI Octobris, A. D. MDCCCLXVI, Habiti, et a Sede Apostolica Recogniti, Acta et Decreta* (Baltimorae: Joannes Murphy, 1868) (hereafter cited *Acta*); cf. also I Provincial Council of Baltimore (1829), Decr. XXV — *Collectio Lacensis*, III, 30-31.

nitentiae ministrandum est in locis sacris ad id destinatis.[72] The I Diocesan Synod of Utrecht (1867) said that such a good reason was verified in the case of clerics, whose confession could licitly be heard in any fitting place, even at home.[73]

In 1869 the Sacred Congregation for the Propagation of the Faith repeated a prohibition against hearing the confessions of women before dawn and after dusk, and cited the original decree given in this regard by the Sacred Congregation of Bishops and Regulars on June 21, 1620.[74]

The Vicar of Rome had received notice that within his jurisdiction certain churches and religious institutes, especially of women, did not have proper confessionals. Accordingly the following regulations were issued on February 9, 1898, to all the rectors of churches, and to the superiors of monasteries and religious houses in Rome. The rectors of churches, in order to forestall abuses which could give rise to very serious inconveniences, were to remember that the confessionals for women should be placed in an open place in church and equipped with an immovable screen, preferably covered with some sort of veil, and constructed in such a way as to leave the confessor completely separated from the penitent. Women's confessionals located in the sacristy, or having no fixed grating, or those which, though located in the church, nevertheless were in a place set apart, dark, and nearly hidden from public view, and also those which consisted of a simple table with grating, the so-called "half-confessionals," were all to be considered as irregular. Also irregular were the confessionals in monasteries and religious houses of women which, though having a fixed grating, did not have a veil which rendered it impossible to see the confessor, and those in which the confessor did not remain in a compartment different from that of the penitent. Even in proper confessionals in the churches the confessions of women were not to be heard later than a half hour

---

72. Cap. VIII — *Collectio Lacensis,* V, 830; cf. also I Provincial Council of New Granada (1868), Cap. VIII — *Collectio Lacensis,* VI, 514-5.

73. *Acta et Statuta Primae Synodi Dioecesanae Ultrajectensis* (Gestel St. Michaelis, 1867), p. 49.

74. *Collectanea S. Congregationis de Propaganda Fide* (2 vols., Romae: Typographia Polyglotta, S. C. de Propaganda Fide, 1907), n. 1339.

after the evening *Angelus,* unless by some very special privilege their confessions could be heard at a later hour.[75]

The Diocesan Synod of Lucca (1887) required each church to have a confessional equipped with a screen and located in a patent, apt, and conspicuous place. To hear women's confessions outside such a place implied a grave violation and subjected the confessor to penalties to be imposed at the discretion of the ordinary.[76]

The Plenary Council of Latin America (1899), held in Rome, merely tolerated the practice of hearing in private homes the confessions of men who could not go to the ordinary *locus sacer.* And if women were heard at home, there was always to be a screen or barrier between the confessor and the penitent.[77]

Van der Stappen bore witness to the practices in vogue in the Diocese of Malines. He mentioned that confessions could be heard outside the church for a good reason such as the infirmity of the confessor or of the penitent. The sacristy or any other place contiguous to the church was to be used only for those who were hard of hearing and those who could not confess in the usual place in church. The confessions of women could not licitly be heard outside the confessional in church except in a case of necessity, and then with these precautions: if in a private home, the place was to be open as much as possible and the door of the room left ajar; if in the sacristy, a grille was to be used and the door was to be left open so that both the confessor and the penitent could be seen. A confessor could never under any pretext, not even to impose sacramental penance which he forgot to enjoin or because of an omitted sin, hear the confession, in whole or in part, of a woman just outside the confessional. In extraordinary circumstances, as in the case of a large congregation of people, temporary confessionals could be used, but they were to have the following necessary elements: a seat for the confessor, and for the penitent a prie-dieu equipped with a perforated grating separating the confessor from the penitent.[78]

---

75. *Analecta Ecclesiastica* (Romae, 1893-1911), VI (1898), 247.

76. *Lucanae Ecclesiae Synodus Dioecesana* (Lucae, 1887), p. 120, § II, XIII-XIV.

77. *Acta et Decreta Concilii Plenarii Americae Latinae Anno 1889 Romae Celebrati* (2 vols., Romae, 1902), I, § 239, n. 549.

78. Van der Stappen, *Sacra Liturgia* (5 vols., Vol. IV, Mechliniae, 1900), IV, nn. 127-131.

In the United States diocesan synods followed very closely in their decrees the regulations of the II Plenary Council of Baltimore (1866). They enjoined upon pastors an obligation in conscience to be vigilant in the administration of the sacrament of penance. The pastors were to erect as many confessionals in the church as were necessary, and locate them in an open and conspicuous place. Only in cases of infirmity or necessity could they hear confessions in homes, always, however, leaving the door of the room open.[79]

The III Diocesan Synod of Albany (1884) decreed that during retreats, missions, and Forty Hours, a sufficient number of confessionals, equipped with *crates,* were to be provided for the hearing of women's confessions.[80]

---

79. Cf. *Synodus Dioecesana Chicagiensis Prima, Juxta Normam a Conc. Balt. III Praestitutam, Habita in Ecclesia Metropolitana S. S. Nominis* (Chicagiae, 1887), tit. XIV, n. 155; *Decreta Synodorum Hartfordiensium in unum volumen Collecta* (Hartfordiae, 1902), I, p. 19, n. 8; II, p. 47, n. 35; III, p. 95, n. 92; *Synodus Dioecesana Neo-Eboracensis Quarta Quae Antecedentium etiam Complectitur Constitutiones, Diebus VIII et IX Nov. A. D. 1882, in Ecclesia Metropolitana S. Patritii, Neo-Eboraci Habita* (Neo Eboraci, 1882), cap. IV, n. III; *Acta Synodi Roffensis Tertiae Quam die IX Junii 1914 in Ecclesia Cathedrali S. Patricii Roffae* [*Episcopus*] *celebravit* (Roffae, 1914), cap. IV, § VI, n. 307; *Statuta Dioeceseos Trentonensis Quae in Synodo Dioecesana Secunda die Vigesima Quinta Mensis Junii A. D. 1896 in Ecclesia Cathedrali Beatae Mariae Virgini Dicata Trentonii Habita* (Trentonii, 1897), cap. V, n. 108; *Constitutiones Synodorum Dioecesanarum Sanctae Fidei Novi Mexici Primae, Secundae et Tertiae Quae Habitae fuerunt* (Las Vegas, 1893), cap. III, § 4, n. 3; *Statuta Dioeceseos Pittsburgensis in Synodis Dioecesanis, Habitis Annis Domini 1844, 1846, 1856, 1858, 1869, lata et prout nunc prostant promulgata in Synodo Dioecesana Sexta, Diebus 7, 8 et 9 Februarii 1893* Habita (Pittsburg, 1893), cap. VI, n. 15; *Synodus Dioecesana Syracusana Prima Die XIV Sept. A. D. 1887, in Ecclesia Sanctae Mariae in Coelos Assumptae Syracusis Habita* (New York, 1887), tit. XIV, n. 155; *Acta et Statuta Synodi Richmondiensis Secundae Mense Aug. A. D. 1886 Celebratae* (Baltimorae, 1886), n. 76; *Synodus Dioecesana Wheelingensis Quarta Quae Antecedentium etiam Complectitur Constitutiones Diebus 9 et 10 Aug. A. D. 1882 Habita* (Wheelingii, 1882), n. LXXIII.

80. *Synodus Dioecesana Albanensis Tertia Quae Antecedentium etiam Complectitur Constitutiones, Diebus VI et VII Februarii A. D. 1884 in Seminario S. Josephi Habita* (New York, 1884), cap. XI, n. 84.

E. TWENTIETH CENTURY

It is not necessary to mention any councils or synods in the few pre-Code years of this century, since the trend already was sufficiently established to indicate no departure from the accepted regulations and practice concerning the hearing of confessions. It remained for the Code of Canon Law to take the substantial elements from the decrees of the Sacred Congregations and to formulate them into canons 908-910.

ARTICLE 2. *The Place for the Hearing of the Confessions of Nuns*

Since the place for the hearing of confessions is of special importance in the case of nuns, this aspect is worthy of separate treatment. That the laws concerning the cloister of nuns, especially those subject to regulars, were very strict and severe is attested by the fact that, in the statutes of certain Nuns of St. Dominic, no mention was made of the confessor's being permitted to enter the cloister to hear the confession of a sick nun. Yet, permission was granted for the administration of Holy Viaticum and extreme unction. When a doubt arose in the matter, Pope Clement VII (1523-1534) in an apostolic letter under date of January 5, 1532, granted the confessor permission to enter the cloister if the nun's illness was dangerous. The confessor, however, was to administer the Holy Eucharist at the same time in order not to multiply his entrances into the cloister.[81]

The Sacred Congregation of Bishops and Regulars decreed on September 13, 1583, that a confessor could enter a sick nun's cell to hear her confession, but that two nuns were to accompany him and remain standing at the open cell door, within easy sight, but not within earshot, of both the penitent and the confessor.[82] If the nun was able to go to the confessional, the confessor could not hear her in the cloister.[83] According to this same decree a secular confessor needed no male companion when he entered a nun's cell.[84] Later, however, according to

81. *Benedicti XIV Pont. Op. Max. olim Prosperi Card. de Lambertinis Institutiones Ecclesiasticae* (12 vols., Romae, 1747-1751), XI, 187-8.

82. Cited in Pellizzari, *Tractatio De Monialibus* (3. ed., Venetiis, 1651), p. 439 (hereafter cited *De Monialibus*).

83. Ferraris, *Prompta Bibliotheca*, s. v. *Confessarius*, art. IV, n. 58.

84. Maupied, *Iuris Canonici Compendium* (2 vols., Parisiis, 1863), II, 235.

Ferraris (+ ca. 1763), regular confessors, notwithstanding any old customs, could not enter without a companion over fifty years of age and of exemplary character.[85] On September 22, 1592, the Sacred Congregation of Bishops and Regulars stated that the confessional for nuns was to be located in church.[86]

The Sacred Congregation of the Council in 1605 ordered the confessionals of nuns to be removed from sacristies and secluded places and to be located in the outer church. And in 1617 it repeated this command, adding that nuns who did not comply would be interdicted.[87] In commenting on this prescription, Pellizzari (1596-1651) explained that if necessity demanded, as for example when there was only one confessional in the church and both the ordinary and extraordinary confessors were going to hear confessions at the same time, then, because of the excusing necessity, it was licit to hear confessions in another place; but even then it was necessary that the place be such *ut mutuus vitetur aspectus confessarii ac monialis confitentis*.[88]

In 1617 when the Sacred Congregation of the Council was asked whether the confessionals of nuns could be located in sacristies or in the house in which the confessor lived, it replied in the negative, and required them to be placed in the churches of the monasteries.[89] According to Wigandt (+1708), a confessor could enter a nun's cell to hear her confession when she was in danger of death; and even outside such danger he could for a grave and just reason hear her confession in a parlor or some similar place, but he was always to be outside the cloister.[90] The reason was that such a great necessity knew no law, and the cause excused if it was judged by the superior to be grave. In 1642 the Sacred Congregation of the Council was asked whether the confessionals of nuns could be located in sacristies or in the homes of confessors, especially if they could conveniently be placed in churches.

---

85. *Prompta Bibliotheca,* s. v. *Moniales,* art. V, n. 65.

86. S. C. Ep. et Reg., *Vicentina,* 22 sept. 1592 — *Fontes,* n. 1464.

87. Cited by Ferraris, *Prompta Bibliotheca,* s. v. *Confessarius,* art. IV, n. 69.

88. Pellizzari, *De Monialibus,* p. 439.

89. S. C. C., 2 sept. 1617, ad 4 — *Fontes,* n. 2405; cf. also S. C. C., *Salutiarum,* 20 sept. 1642, ad 7 — *Fontes,* n. 2637.

90. Wigandt, *Tribunal Confessariorum et Ordinandorum* (Venetiis, 1717), p. 548 (hereafter cited *Tribunal Confessariorum*).

Again, as in 1617, it replied that they could not, but had to be located in the churches of the monasteries.[91]

In 1682, in an encyclical letter issued by the Sacred Congregation of Bishops and Regulars, Pope Innocent XI (1676-1689) restated the requirement for confessors to have two accompanying nuns stand at the open door whenever they heard a sick nun's confession in her cell.[92]

On October 20, 1664, Pope Alexander VII (1655-1667) in his Constitution *Felici* had clearly defined the right of regular confessors to enter the cloister:

> Furthermore, the confessor of nuns, both ordinary and extraordinary, shall by no means enter the cloister of the monastery except to administer the sacraments of penance, of the Holy Eucharist, and of extreme unction to the nuns or other sick persons dwelling there, and to assist the dying; nor shall he enter at all except with a companion, who must be of exemplary life and mature age, and who must remain in such a part of the monastery where he can always see the confessor and be seen by him.[93]

Whenever a confessor entered the cloister of nuns, he was expected to enter and return by a direct and not a roundabout way. He could not visit other parts of the convent, even for the sake of other sick nuns, as long as they were not in need of receiving the sacraments.[94]

Once the confessor had finished his ministrations, he was not to delay more than a minute or two, and certainly not more than a quarter of an hour. Nevertheless, if he delayed a little longer than necessary, he did not incur any censure for violation of the cloister, since this penalty was intended only for those who entered without permission. Since the penal character of the law was an odious matter, its application was not to be extended to those who entered with permission, even though they abused that permission to a slight extent.[95]

---

91. S. C. C., *Salutiarum,* 20 sept. 1642, ad 7 — *Fontes,* n. 2637.
92. Cited by Ferraris, *Prompta Bibliotheca,* s. v. *Confessarius,* art. IV, n. 56.
93. Alexander VII, const. *Felici,* 20 oct. 1664 — *Fontes,* n. 240. Translation by the writer.
94. Pellizzari, *De Monialibus,* p. 439.
95. Wigandt, *Tribunal Confessariorum,* p. 180.

A decree of the Sacred Congregation of the Council in 1727 allowed the bishop and both the ordinary and extraordinary confessor to enter the monastery without restriction, as often as they were called by a sick nun who desired to make her confession out of mere devotion.[96]

Dom Bastien (1866-1940) was of the opinion that, although all this legislation regarding the confessional was intended for nuns, that is, for women religious professed with solemn vows, the reasons which prompted it were verified equally well in the case of women religious professed with simple vows. Therefore, if they had but one chapel in their religious house, the confessional was to be placed in the chapel in such a manner as to make both the confessor and the penitent easily visible.[97]

The Sacred Congregation of the Holy Office in 1874 was asked three questions regarding the place for the hearing of nuns' confessions: (1) Were the places in which the confessions of nuns were customarily heard to be considered as places destined for the hearing of confessions, or, in other words, as true confessionals? (2) Was the same thing to be said about the confessionals in which were heard the confessions of women who resided at training institutes (*conservatoria*) or retreat houses, as long as the confessionals were constructed according to the same form as those in which the confessions of cloistered nuns were usually heard? (3) If they were to be considered as true confessionals, were they such only in regard to nuns and other women living in the aforementioned places, or even in regard to outside women? To all three questions an affirmative answer was given.[98]

With regard to the confessions which women religious made to an occasional confessor, the early concessions of this privilege made no mention of the element of place. The first decree emanated from the Sacred Congregation of Bishops and Regulars under date of August 27, 1852.[99] It stated that nuns who, retaining the habit, were outside their convent for a short time for their health or any other reason could go

96. S. C. C., *in Mazariensi,* 10 maii 1727, as cited in *Benedicti XIV Omnia Opera* (17 vols. in 18, Prati, 1829-1847), XIII, 263-265.

97. *Directoire Canonique à L'Usage des Congrégations à Voeux Simples* (Abbaye de Maredsous, 1904), p. 218.

98. S. C. S. Off., 25 nov. 1874 — *Fontes,* n. 1033.

99. S. C. Ep. et Reg., 27 aug. 1852 — *Fontes,* n. 1964.

to confession to any priest approved by the ordinary for both sexes, even though he was not approved for the confessions of nuns. This restriction concerning the habit, the reason for being outside and the length of their stay outside were not prescribed in the case of school sisters who used this permission. Sisters who, though they were outside the enclosure, lived the common life and received the sacraments in the parish church, since they had no chapel of their own, could go to confession outside their house to any confessor approved by the ordinary.[100]

The statutes of the archdiocese of Malines and of the diocese of Tournai allowed nuns who were outside the convent to go to confession in churches to any priest approved for the confessions of both sexes. A decree from the Sacred Penitentiary on February 9, 1901, declared that such confessions were valid.[101]

The Sacred Congregation of Religious in the decree *Cum de sacramentalibus* on February 3, 1913, gave nuns and sisters outside their convent for any reason the right to go to confession not only in churches but even in oratories, including semi-public oratories.[102]

ARTICLE 3. *Confessions in Oratories*

The V Provincial Council of Milan (1579) issued a decree stating that, except for illness or urgent necessity, confessions, even those of men, were not to be heard outside a church or an oratory.[103] But it is predominantly from the eighteenth century that most of the decrees concerning the hearing of confessions in oratories emanated. A decree was issued by the Sacred Congregation of Rites in 1710, which decree, in deciding the primary point at issue, namely, whether a certain Confraternity of St. Joseph was permitted to retain a confessional in its oratory for the hearing of confessions therein without the permission of the pastor within whose limits the oratory was situated, stated that the matter was to be left to the discretion of the ordinary. That was

100. S. C. Ep. et Reg., *Atrebaten.*, 22 apr. 1872, ad 3 — *Fontes*, n. 2000.

101. Cf. Vermeersch, *De Religiosis Institutis et Personis Tractatus Canonico-Moralis* (2 vols., Vol. II, 4. ed., Brugis, 1909), II, n. 233.

102. S. C. de Religiosis, decr. *Cum de sacramentalibus*, 3 febr. 1913 — *Acta Apostolicae Sedis, Commentarium Officiale* (Romae, 1909-), V (1913), 64 (hereafter cited *AAS*); *Fontes*, n. 4416.

103. Cap. X — Mansi, XXXIV A, 367-368.

sufficient to indicate that with the ordinary's permission confessions could be heard in an oratory. However, nothing was said to indicate what type of oratory was in question.[104]

In 1714 the same Sacred Congregation of Rites informed the Congregation of the Oratory of St. Philip Neri that it could retain in the chapels of its various houses a confessional for the public hearing of the confessions of the faithful of both sexes without the pastor's, but with the bishop's, permission. The question here again turned about an oratory, evidently a public one.[105]

In response to a question, namely, whether the chaplains of a particular confraternity could hear the confessions of the brothers, and even of women and others, the Sacred Congregation of the Council in 1743 replied in the affirmative, provided that the permission of the ordinary was obtained, to the exclusion, however, of women's confessions.[106] In all these questions the fundamental point involved was the necessity of the ordinary's permission. Yet, secondarily, they clearly indicated the frequent use of the oratory as a place for the hearing of confessions.

In 1744 the same Sacred Congregation was asked to decide whether a particular oratory was public or private, and also whether it was permissible to retain a confessional there. It replied that the oratory in question was to be considered public, yet confessions, but not those of women, were to be heard only with the abbot's permission.[107]

The Sacred Congregation of the Council in 1757 gave a similar reply involving a "simple" or private oratory.[108] Thus it is easily seen

---

104. S. R. C., *Placentina,* 22 nov. 1710—*Fontes,* n. 5746; cf. also S. R. C., 9 mart. 1711, ad 3—*Decreta Authentica Congregationis Sacrorum Rituum ex actis eiusdem collecta eiusque auctoritate promulgata sub auctoritate SS. Domini nostri Leonis Papae XIII* (6 vols., Romae: Ex Typographia Polyglotta S. C. de Prop. Fid., 1898-1927), n. 2210 (hereafter cited *Decr. Auth.*).

105. S. R. C., 10 mart. 1714, ad 7—*Decr. Auth.,* n. 2224; cf. also S. R. C., 9 iul. 1718, ad 1 et 2—*Decr. Auth.,* n. 2251.

106. S. C. C., 12 aug. 1743—*Thesaurus Resolutionum Sacrae Congregationis Concilii* (167 vols., Romae, 1718-1908), LI, 135-136 (hereafter cited *Thesaurus*).

107. S. C. C., *Nullius seu Nonantulana,* 13 et 27 iun. 1744—*Fontes,* n. 3566.

108. S. C. C., *in Cassanen.,* 12 aug. 1757—Pallottini, *Collectio,* s. v. *Sacramentum Poenitentiae,* n. 112.

that a public oratory in no way *ipso facto* implied the right to set up a confessional, nor did the fact that an oratory was private exclude the possibility of its having a confessional.

As regards public oratories, De Bonis (+ after 1761) attested the fact that in the Archdiocese of Milan it was the custom everywhere to hear confessions in them, he himself having done so many times. As long as the priest was approved for the hearing of confessions and had the permission of the pastor, the sacrament of penance could be administered in any public oratory.[109]

In two decrees under dates of August 20, 1761, and May 8, 1762, the Sacred Congregation of the Council decided a question concerning granges (*granciae*), that is, rural rest houses belonging to religious. It decreed that the permission which had been granted before the Council of Trent for the construction of such rural houses did not imply, after the Council, the permission also to have an oratory, and much less the permission to hear there the confessions of those who were in the employ of the monastery, or of other persons who tarried there as visitors.[110]

In 1785 the Sacred Congregation for the Propagation of the Faith was asked if its decree which required a confessional grating for the confessions of women was intended as applicable law only in a permanently erected oratory, and if, when a missionary was obliged to hear a woman's confession in a private home inasmuch as such an oratory was wanting, it was sufficient to have her cover her face with a veil. The simple reply was in the affirmative to both questions, as long as a closer adherence to the law could not be implemented.[111]

Ferraris considered it a very common doctrine that confessions could be heard in private oratories if this was not expressly prohibited by some special constitution.[112] But regarding regulars, Pallottini was of the opinion that they were forbidden to administer the sacrament in

---

109. De Bonis, *De Oratoriis Publicis Tractatus Historico-Canonicus* (Mediolani, 1761), p. 58.

110. S. C. C., in *Toletana,* 20 aug. 1761 et 8 mâii 1762 — Pallottini, *Collectio,* s. v. *Sacramentum Poenitentiae,* n. 118.

111. S. C. de Prop. Fide (C. P. pro Sin. — Chan-si), 17 mart. 1785 — *Fontes,* n. 4600.

112. *Prompta Bibliotheca,* s. v. *Oratorium,* n. 45.

private oratories, even if these had been set up by apostolic authority. He offered two reasons: (1) with reference to the element of place, the Roman Ritual ruled that outside the cases of necessity the sacraments, especially the Holy Eucharist and penance, were to be administered in a church, and not in private oratories; and (2) as touching the persons involved, laymen who did not live within the precincts of the monastery or were not in the employ of the regulars and under obedience to the superior were not exempt from the jurisdiction of the pastor.[113]

ARTICLE 4. *Confessions on Voyages*

The question of hearing confessions at sea is one that primarily involves the problem of jurisdiction, that is, whether the priest possesses the necessary faculties. However, since it also concerns the question of place for the hearing of confessions, at least considered in its broader aspects, its treatment rightfully finds a place in this work.

The Sacred Congregation of the Holy Office, in a decree under date of March 17, 1869,[114] mentioned that this subject had been controverted among theologians, and that there was no unanimity among the doctors or the Roman Sacred Congregations. Hence it is readily seen why the Holy Office was asked whether priests, when undertaking an ocean trip, could be given faculties by the ordinary of the port of departure to hear the confessions of the faithful during the trip. The reply was as follows:

> Posse sacerdotes iter arripientes, ab Ordinariis locorum, unde naves solvunt, adprobari, ita ut, itinere perdurante, fidelium secum navigantium confessiones valide et licite excipere valeant, usquedum perveniant ad locum, ubi alius superior ecclesiasticus iurisdictione pollens constitutus sit.

In order to settle further doubts raised in this matter, the Sacred Congregation of the Holy Office on April 9, 1900, declared that any

113. *Collectio,* s. v. *Sacramentum Poenitentiae,* n. 117.

114. *Collectanea S. Congregationis de Propaganda Fide,* n. 1343; *Fontes,* n. 1009.

priests making an ocean trip, provided that they had faculties from their own ordinary to hear confessions, could hear the confessions of any of the faithful making the voyage with them. And they could do this throughout the whole trip, even though the ship passed through or even docked in different places subject to the jurisdiction of various ordinaries.[115]

In a decree under date of August 23, 1905, it was explained by the Holy Office that the use of this faculty was restricted to the hearing of confessions simply on board ship.[116] The following year, on December 13, the Sacred Congregation of the Holy Office extended the faculty to include not only any of the faithful who for any reason came aboard the ship when it had put up at a port, but also any who approached the priest while he was on shore. In such cases he could validly and licitly absolve from censures reserved to the local ordinary, provided that there was present only one approved confessor or none at all, and provided that the ordinary could not easily be reached.[117]

The Sacred Congregation for the Propagation of the Faith on June 27, 1914, declared the import of these two latter decrees as extending also to the islands in the lakes and rivers of the Upper Congo. Any priests approved by the ordinaries of those missions, if they came to the aforesaid islands, could hear sacramental confessions there, according to the provisions of the decree of December 13, 1906, regarding a priest who in the course of his navigation went ashore.[118]

ARTICLE 5. *Confession* in Absentia

In regard to confession *in absentia,* Medina (1490-1546) considered it probable that, if a penitent could not approach a confessor and the latter could not come to him, the confession could be made by letter

115. *Collectanea S. Congregationis de Propaganda Fide,* n. 2082; *Fontes,* n. 1238.

116. *Collectanea S. Congregationis de Propaganda Fide,* n. 2244; *Fontes,* n. 1275.

117. *Collectanea S. Congregationis de Propaganda Fide,* n. 2244; *Fontes,* n. 1281.

118. Bouscaren, *The Canon Law Digest* (2 vols., Milwaukee: Bruce Publishing Company, 1934-43), II, 219.

or messenger to such an absent confessor, and he in turn could also give sacramental absolution.[119] There could be no objection, he said, against the confession itself, since the making of a written confession was sometimes permitted.

Relative to the absolution he considered three possible objections: (1) the essence of confession demands the vocal, and not merely the written, presentation of one's sins; (2) the very form of sacramental absolution requires the corporal presence of the one absolved; and (3) Christ commanded that the penitent "show himself to the priest."

He ruled out the force of the first objection by pointing out that frequently the absolution from a sentence of excommunication was given in writing. In answer to the second objection he contended that neither the form nor the essence of sacramental absolution required a corporal presence. Likewise the third objection was without force, since Christ did not indicate the necessity of an oral rather than a written absolution. He merely required the cleansed lepers to show themselves to the priest inasfar as that was possible. Thus, if a corporal presence was impossible, there was nothing objectionable in making one's confession through a letter or a messenger. In conclusion, however, though affirming the licitness of such a confession, Medina admitted that it was not necessary under such circumstances. And if a confessor was easily available, confession by letter or messenger was not only illicit but also invalid.

Pope Clement VIII (1592-1605) on July 20, 1602, condemned as at least false, rash and scandalous the proposition which regarded it as licit to confess sacramentally one's sins by letter or messenger to an absent confessor and to receive absolution from the same *in absentia*. Moreover, he forbade that proposition to be taught publicly or privately in any written works or sermons, or also at gatherings. It could never be defended as probable, or be printed or practiced in any way, whether directly or indirectly. Anyone who violated these prohibitions incurred *ipso facto* a censure from which he could not be absolved, except *in articulo mortis*, by anyone other than the Roman Pontiff him-

119. *De Paenitentia, Restitutione, et Contractibus* (Ingolstadii, 1681), pp. 132-133.

self. No other dignitary, not even the major penitentiary, could absolve him. In addition, the violator could be made to undergo other penalties inflicted at the discretion of the proper authority.[120]

ARTICLE 6. *The Place for the Hearing of Confessions in the Oriental Church*

Occasional reference has already been made with regard to the place for the hearing of confessions in the Oriental Church.[121] A few further observations may be made now.

The general practice in the Oriental Church with regard to the place for the hearing of confessions was substantially the same as in the Latin Church. Confessions, as a rule, were to be heard in a confessional[122] placed in an open and conspicuous place in the church.[123] The confessional seat was to be equipped with a perforated screen.[124] In cases of illness[125] and necessity[126] or for any similar reasonable

120. *Bullarii Romani Continuatio,* X, 855; cf. also Barbosa, *De Officio Episcopi,* Pars III, p. 23, n. 163.

121. Cf. Benedictus XIV, const. *Etsi pastoralis,* 26 maii 1742, § V, n. xii — *Bullarii Romani Continuatio,* I, 202; *Fontes,* n. 328; Council of Mt. Lebanon (1736), Pars II, Cap. IV, can. 10 — *Collectio Lacensis,* II, 132; S. C. de Prop. Fide, decr. 13 apr. 1807, n. xiii — *Fontes,* n. 4691; Gregorius XVI, ep. encycl. *Inter gravissimas,* 3 febr. 1832 — *Fontes,* n. 483.

122. Cf. Graeco-Melkite Council (1835), Can. 4, n. 1 — *Collectio Lacensis,* II, 582; Synod of Lemberg (1891), Tit. II, Cap. IV, n. 5 — *Codificazione Canonica Orientale, Fonti* (Serie I, 13 vols., Serie II, 16 vols., Series III, 3 vols. in 4, Città del Vaticano: Tipografia Polyglotta Vaticana, 1930-), Serie I, XI, n. 150 (hereafter cited *Fonti*); Text of the sources of the Syro-Malankarese Canon Law, Cap. XVII, n. iii — *Fonti,* Serie II, IX, n. 531.

123. Cf. I Provincial Rumanian Council (1872), Tit. V, Can. 5 — *Fonti,* Serie I, X, n. 395; Maronite Council of Mt. Lebanon (1736), Pars II, Cap. IV, can. 10 — *Collectio Lacensis,* II, 132.

124. Cf. in the Melkite Rite the Constitutions of St. Basil the Great, Pars II, Cap. V, n. vi — Mansi, XLVI, 1251; Maronite Council of Mt. Lebanon (1736), Pars II, Cap. IV, can. 10 — *Collectio Lacensis,* II, 132.

125. Cf. Graeco-Melkite Council (1835), Canon 4, n. 1 — *Collectio Lacensis,* II, 582.

126. Cf. Maronite Synod of Mt. Lebanon (1736), Pars II, Cap. I, Can. 6 — *Fonti,* Serie I, XII, n. 1372.

cause[127] confessions could be heard outside the confessional seat, but always in an open and decent place.[128] Confessions were not to be heard in a private home except for a reasonable cause such as illness, in which case the door of the room was to be left open.[129]

If the confessions of women were heard not in an open and conspicuous place in the church with a screen interposed between the confessor and the penitent, or if the confessions of women were heard in private homes without a sufficient reason, a penalty was inflicted upon the priest.[130]

As regards the confessions of nuns, the confessor was allowed to enter the monastery only in urgent necessity or because of the nun's infirmity. He was always to be accompanied into the monastery by a male companion of upright character and of mature age, and they were always to be within sight of each other. The confessor was to be accompanied to the cell of the sick nun by the abbess, or her substitute, or by two other nuns as well as the confessor's male companion.[131]

With regard to the visitation of their subjects made by Oriental ordinaries, a Provincial Ruthenian Synod (1720) pointed out the questions that were to be asked: whether the sacrament was administered by day in the confessional; whether the confessional was equipped with a perforated screen; whether the confessions of women and girls were heard outside the confessional seat without a screen interposed between the confessor and the penitent, a thing which was forbidden.[132]

---

127. Cf. S. C. de Prop. Fide, decr. 13 apr. 1807, n. xiii — *Fontes,* n. 4691.

128. Cf. Maronite Council of Mt. Lebanon (1736), Pars II, Cap. IV, can. 10 — *Collectio Lacensis,* II, 132.

129. Cf. S. C. de Prop. Fide, decr. 13 apr. 1807, n. xiii — *Fontes,* n. 4691; Maronite Council of Mt. Lebanon (1836), Pars II, Cap. IV, can 10 — *Collectio Lacensis,* II, 132.

130. Pope Pius IX in a decree which he issued to the Maronites under date of February 18, 1851, enacted in such cases a suspension from the exercise of orders, which suspension was incurred *ipso facto,* and could be lifted only by the apostolic delegate or the patriarch of the country. Cf. *Fonti,* Serie I, I, 103-105.

131. Cf. Maronite Council of Mt. Lebanon (1736), Pars IV, Cap. III, can. 14 — *Collectio Lacensis,* II, 381-382.

132. *Collectio Lacensis,* II, 70.

These examples, though by no means as copious as the examples that have been given of legislation in the Latin Church, seem to the writer sufficient to compel the conclusion that there was no substantial difference between the Oriental and the Latin Churches with regard to the place for the hearing of confessions.

Part Two

CANONICAL COMMENTARY

Chapter III

THE GENERAL RULE AS REGARDS PLACE

The general rule as regards the place for the hearing of sacramental confessions is that they are to be heard in a church, a public or a semi-public oratory. This norm is stated in canon 908: *Sacramentalis confessionis proprius locus est ecclesia vel oratorium publicum aut semi-publicum.* It is to be observed ordinarily as regards the confessions of both men and women. It is certain from canon 909, § 2, that such confessions are to be heard ordinarily in a confessional seat, constructed according to the prescriptions enacted in this same canon, that is to say, one which is equipped with a fixed grating perforated with small openings: *Sedes confessionalis crate fixa ac tenuiter perforata inter poenitentem et confessarium sit instructa.* Furthermore, according to canon 909, § 1, for the confessions of women the confessional seat is always to be located in an open and conspicuous place, and generally in a church, or in a public or semi-public oratory destined for women: *Sedes confessionalis ad audiendas mulierum confessiones semper collocetur in loco patenti et conspicuo, et generatim in ecclesia vel oratorio publico aut semi-publico mulieribus destinato.*

Article 1. *The Proper Place for the Hearing of Confessions*

Canon 908 speaks of the proper place for the hearing of confessions. In general parlance a proper place is one in which an act is performed by way of its usual and customary performance. Outside its proper place an action is performed only rarely and by way of exception. To explain this, Maroto (1875-1937) gives the example of a bed. This is considered to be the proper place in which to sleep, since one ordinarily sleeps in a bed. However, under unusual or extraordinary circumstances one may find it necessary to sleep elsewhere.[1]

In regard to the hearing of confessions, the proper place is that in which by common rule and practice the faithful, both men and women, confess their sins. According to the prescription of canon 908 such a place must be a church, or a public or semi-public oratory. The reason for the selection of these places as proper places for the hearing of confessions lies in the fact that they are in general sacred places. In the strict canonical sense of the term, sacred places are defined as those which are set aside by a liturgical blessing or consecration for divine worship or of the burial of the faithful.[2] As Cappello says, it is fitting that the ordinary place for the administration of a sacrament should be a sacred place. Therefore he rules out private oratories, and *a fortiori* private homes, as proper places for the hearing of confessions, precisely for the reason that they are not sacred places.[3]

The mere fact, however, that a place is a sacred place does not make it automatically a proper place for the hearing of confessions. For there are sacred places besides churches, public and semi-public oratories, which, though they are sacred in the strict canonical sense, are not proper places for the hearing of confessions.[4] In order to be a proper place for the administration or reception of the sacraments, a place must be recognized as such by the law.

On the other hand, the sacraments may be received or administered even in places which are not sacred places in the strict canonical sense of the term, i. e., under such circumstances for which the law has made due provision. Thus confessions may be heard in places other than those named in canon 908, provided that the prescriptions of the law are observed.

The Church designates the places which are to be considered as the proper places for the administration and the reception of the sacra-

1. Maroto, "De Loco ad Confessiones Excipiendas," *Apollinaris* (Romae: 1928-), I (1928), 408.

2. Cf. canon 1154.

3. Cappello, *Tractatus Canonico-Moralis de Sacramentis* (3 vols. in 6, Vol. II, *De Poenitentia,* 3. ed., Taurinorum Augustae: Marietti, 1938), II, n. 939 (hereafter cited *De Poenitentia*).

4. Cf. canon 1154.

ments, except, for obvious reasons, in respect of the sacrament of extreme unction, which must often be administered to one who is found in abject circumstances. Those proper places, under ordinary circumstances, are sacred places.[5]

Outside those places which are specified by the Church as proper places for the administration of the sacraments it is not permitted to administer or receive the sacraments except in certain cases, provided the prescriptions of the law are observed. The degree of severity of this prohibition, however, varies in the case of the various sacraments. Hence the circumstance of place cannot be urged with equal rigor in all cases.[6] Yet even in those exceptional cases the place chosen must always be such as befits the dignity of the sacrament which is administered or received therein.

It will be advantageous to examine here what the Church's prescriptions are in regard to the proper place for the administration of the various sacraments. As regards baptism, while it is true that in an urgent necessity private baptism may be administered in any place,[7] nevertheless the proper place for the administration of solemn baptism is a church or public oratory.[8] Solemn baptism may be administered in private homes only with legitimate permission and under closely specified circumstances.[9] The proper place for the administration of the sacrament of confirmation is a church. Nevertheless, the minister may confer this sacrament in any other fitting place if he has a reason which he judges to be both just and good.[10] Ordinarily it is necessary to celebrate the Holy Sacrifice of the Mass in a church or an oratory which is blessed or consecrated.[11]

For the celebration of Mass outside these places one must have the legitimate permission of the ordinary, which, however, cannot be

---

5. Maroto, "De Loco ad Confessiones Excipiendas," *Apollinaris,* I (1928), 408.

6. Cappello, *De Poenitentia,* II, n. 939; cf. also Maroto, "De Loco ad Confessiones Excipiendas," *Apollinaris,* I (1928), 408.

7. Cf. canon 771.

8. Cf. canon 773.

9. Cf. canon 776.

10. Cf. canon 791.

11. Cf. canon 822, § 1.

granted except for a just and good reason in some extraordinary case and by way of individual grant, that is, as long as the condition which necessitates the exception continues.[12] Holy Communion may be distributed wherever the Holy Sacrifice of the Mass is offered, even in a private oratory, unless the local ordinary forbids it for a just reason in some particular case.[13] Sacred orders are always to be conferred in a church or oratory; only first tonsure and minor orders may be conferred in a private oratory.[14] Marriages are to be celebrated in a church, or in a public or semi-public oratory. Exceptions from this rule are to be made only for a just and good reason in an extraordinary case or in the case of a mixed marriage.[15]

With regard to the sacrament of penance, the proper place for the hearing of confessions is a church, or a public or semi-public oratory. Ordinarily, then, confessions are to be heard in these places. But a general rule is simply a rule which finds its application as long as happenings and events conform to their usual pattern, and therefore such a rule necessarily leaves room for exceptions. Yet in order to deviate from the general requirement to hear confessions in a church, or in a public or semi-public oratory, one must have a good reason which stands verified in the light of the exceptional circumstances.

It is to be noted that the legislator does not exclude from the hearing of confessions the places which are not mentioned in canon 908. It is merely stated as a positive, but not as an exclusive, assertion that the places mentioned therein are proper places for the administration of the sacrament of penance. Though they are designated in the law as the proper places, there are also other places which by way of tolerance can offer the due propriety. Therefore the explicitly designated proper places may be described as reflecting the law's preference rather than as connoting the law's insistence on a completely exclusive choice of places.[16]

---

12. Cf. canon 822, § 4.
13. Cf. canon 869.
14. Cf. canon 1009.
15. Cf. canon 1109.
16. Regatillo, *Ius Sacramentarium* (2 vols., Vol. I, Santander: Sal Terrae, 1945), I, n. 668.

ARTICLE 2. *Churches as Proper Places for the Hearing of Confessions*

In order to understand what is implied in a proper place for the hearing of confessions it is necessary to consider the canonical nature of a church and of the various types of oratories. Canon 1161 defines a church as a sacred edifice dedicated to divine worship primarily to the end that it may serve all the faithful for their public exercise of that worship.[17]

Churches, then, are for the use of the faithful in general in their public exercise of divine worship. Though some oratories are open also to the public, they are intended fundamentally for the convenience of a particular community or for the promotion of a special work. This constitutes the primary difference between a church and an oratory, for the definition of a church and an oratory, as formulated in the Code, directly contrasts them one to the other. Even in the case of a public oratory, when the law recognizes an equal right for all the faithful, the oratory is primarily intended for a particular group of persons and only secondarily for all the faithful.[18]

In the definition of a church the phrase "divine worship" includes all sacred functions, inclusive of the preaching of the word of God. However, the writer's interest is limited to the administration of the sacrament of penance. The following list includes the various kinds of churches: 1) basilicas; 2) cathedral churches; 3) collegiate churches; 4) parochial churches; 5) conventual churches; 6) succursal churches.[19] Any of these churches, therefore, is to be considered as a proper place for the hearing of confessions.

The sacristy is described as that place in the church or adjoining the church in which the sacred vessels and vestments are kept, and in

---

17. "Ecclesiae nomine intelligitur aedes sacra divino cultui dedicata eum potissimum in finem ut omnibus Christifidelibus usui sit ad divinum cultum publice exercendum."

18. Vermeersch-Creusen, *Epitome Iuris Canonici* (6. ed., 3 vols., Mechliniae-Romae: Dessain, 1937-1946), II, n. 475 (hereafter cited *Epitome*); cf. also Regatillo, *Ius Sacramentarium*, I, n. 198.

19. Coronata, *De Locis et Temporibus Sacris* (Augustae Taurinorum: Marietti, 1922), n. 12.

which the celebrant and his ministers vest for the conducting of the divine offices.[20] Although the existence of a sacristy is not prescribed for such uses by any particular canon, nevertheless there should be one in every church. Strictly taken, the sacristy is not a sacred place, for it is neither blessed nor consecrated.[21] It is to be considered not as a part of the church, but as distinct from it. Proof of this is found in the fact that if there be committed in the sacristy any of the acts by which a church can become violated,[22] then the perpetration of these acts will not result in the violation of the church.[23] However, if the sacristy immediately adjoins the church, then in all matters of favorable import for it the sacristy may be regarded as part of the church.[24] More will be said later in regard to the sacristy as a place for the hearing of confessions.

ARTICLE 3. *Public Oratories as Proper Places for the Hearing of Confessions*

Canon 908 expressly mentions public and semi-public oratories as proper places for the hearing of confessions. According to canon 1188 a public oratory is defined as one which is erected principally for the convenience of a collegiate body or even of private individuals, but in such a manner that all the faithful have by law the warranted right to frequent it at least at the time of divine services.[25] The principal difference between a public oratory and a church lies in the fact that such an oratory may be erected for the convenience of private persons or

20. Regatillo, *Institutiones Iuris Canonici* (2 vols., Vol. II, *De Rebus*, Santander: Sal Terrae, 1942), II, n. 13 (hereafter cited *Institutiones*).

21. Coronata, *Institutiones Iuris Canonici* (2. ed., 5 vols., Taurini: Marietti, 1939-1947), II, 25, note 1 (hereafter cited *Institutiones*).

22. Cf. canon 1172, § 1.

23. Coronata, *Institutiones*, II, 50.

24. Regatillo, *Institutiones*, II, n. 13.

25. Canon 1188, § 2, 1°. "Est vero oratorium publicum si praecipue erectum sit in commodum alicuius collegii aut etiam privatorum, ita tamen ut omnibus fidelibus, tempore saltem divinorum officiorum, ius sit, legitime comprobatum, illud adeundi."

for the benefit of a corporation or a collegiate moral person. It is not erected primarily for the benefit of all the faithful, but the latter nevertheless have the legally acknowledged right to frequent it at least at the time of divine services. This is a strict right, and not a favor. There is a corresponding obligation not to interfere in any way with the exercise of this right. Thus the faithful are to have unimpeded access to a public oratory.

According to canon 1188, § 2, 1°, it suffices that the public oratory be open to public approach at the times of divine services. For not even a church needs to be open at all times. The Code does not specify exactly what is to be understood by divine services in this connection. Canon 2256, 1°, states: *In canonibus qui sequuntur: nomine divinorum officiorum intelliguntur functiones potestatis ordinis, quae de instituto Christi vel Ecclesiae ad divinum cultum ordinantur et a solis clericis fieri queunt.* By analogy this definition may be used in the interpretation of canon 1188.[26]

As regards the laws which govern public oratories, canon 1191, § 1, applies to public oratories all the laws that govern churches.[27] From this fact alone it could be argued that a public oratory is a proper place for the hearing of confessions. Valid as this argument is, it receives its fullest confirmation in canon 908, which expressly includes public oratories as proper places for the hearing of confessions. In conclusion, then, any and every public oratory is a proper place in which confessions can lawfully be heard.

It should be noted here that oratories which have a fixed location on ships are public oratories according to a decree of the Sacred Congregation of Rites, issued on March 4, 1901.[28]

---

26. Blat, *Commentarium Textus Codicis Iuris Canonici* (5 vols. in 7, Romae: Ex Typographia Pontificia in Instituto Pii IX, 1921-1938. Lib. I, 1921; Lib. II, ed. altera, 1921; Lib. II, partes II, III, 3. ed., 1938; Lib. III, Pars I, 2. ed. aucta et emendata, 1924; Lib. III, partes II-VI, 2. ed. examinata denuo et aucta, 1934; Lib. IV, 1927; Lib. V, 1924), Lib. III, partes II-VI, n. 40 (hereafter cited *Commentarium*).

27. "Oratoria publica eodem iure quo ecclesiae reguntur."

28. S. R. C., *Vicen.*, 4 mart. 1901, ad 5 — *Decr. Auth.*, n. 4069.

ARTICLE 4. *Semi-public Oratories as Proper Places for the Hearing of Confessions*

Semi-public oratories are also explicitly mentioned in canon 908 as being proper places for the hearing of confessions. By definition, semi-public oratories are those which are erected for the advantage of a certain community or of a group of the faithful gathering there, all others of the faithful lacking the same right to frequent them.[29] The principal difference between a public and a semi-public oratory lies in the fact that the faithful in general have no right to frequent the latter. Therefore they in whose favor the oratory has been erected have an exclusive right to its use. If the faithful in general are nevertheless *de facto* left free to frequent such a semi-public oratory, the concession implies nothing more than an act of gratuitous indulgence in their favor, and it may be withdrawn at will by the community or the group whose direct benefit the oratory serves.

Before an oratory can be established as a semi-public oratory there must be obtained the permission of the ordinary.[30] Before granting this permission, however, the ordinary must visit the oratory personally, or through a delegate who is at least a cleric, and ascertain that it is suitably fitted out and furnished for its intended purpose.[31] Although according to canon 1192, § 4, there ordinarily is to be only one oratory in educational institutions, hospitals, prisons, barracks of soldiers, etc., nevertheless the Code permits the ordinary to allow a plurality of oratories if he deems it necessary or useful. Despite the fact that some authors have referred to these secondary oratories as private oratories, it is evident from the definition of canon 1188 that they are to be considered as semi-public oratories. As semi-public oratories, then, they are proper places for the hearing of confessions.

In the enumeration of institutions as contained in canon 1192, § 4, religious houses are left unmentioned. Vermeersch (1858-1936)-Creusen contend that the manner in which this canon precludes the establishing of more than one oratory at the mentioned institutions, un-

29. Cf. canon 1188, § 2, 2°.
30. Cf. canon 1192, § 1.
31. Cf. canon 1192, § 2.

less the ordinary deems the establishing of two or more oratories either necessary or useful, seems to point to the fact that at religious houses a plurality of oratories can more readily be established.[32] Even though secondary or subsidiary oratories do not come under the definition of canon 1188, § 2, 2°, nevertheless they are to be considered as semi-public oratories because canon 1188, § 2, 2°, which is the only canon that refers to secondary oratories, states that they are to be likened to semi-public oratories. The definition of a private oratory may not be applied to secondary oratories since they are not established in private homes. Therefore secondary oratories in religious houses are also proper places for the hearing of confessions.

Cemetery chapels which belong to a religious community are semi-public chapels; they are neither public nor private. Vermeersch-Creusen state that through the analogy in the law these chapels are to be regarded as semi-public oratories, since the Code classifies as private oratories only those cemetery chapels which belong to private families or individuals.[33] Thus the cemetery chapels of religious communities are likewise to be considered as proper places for the hearing of confessions.

ARTICLE 5. *Private Oratories as Proper Places for the Hearing of Confessions*

There are three classes of private oratories: 1) those which are established in private homes for the convenience of a family or of private individuals; 2) the oratories of cardinals or of bishops; and 3) the oratories which are established in cemeteries. Oratories of the first class are domestic oratories in the strict sense, while those in the second category are private rather than domestic oratories. Inasmuch as canon 1189 states that, although the oratories of cardinals and bishops, both residential and titular, are private oratories, they nevertheless enjoy all the rights and privileges enjoyed by semi-public oratories, they must be regarded as proper places for the hearing of confessions. The other two classes of private oratories mentioned above, precisely because they are private oratories, are not to be considered as proper places for the hearing of confessions. However, the confessions of men may be heard

32. *Epitome*, II, n. 501.
33. *Epitome*, II, n. 499.

in a private oratory; the confessions of women may be heard in a private oratory only in cases of necessity and provided that the prescriptions of canons 909 and 910 are observed. These shall be explained later.

According to canon 1190 cemetery chapels are private oratories.[34] Though such oratories are rather numerous in Europe, they are extremely rare in this country. Whatever chapels are established in cemeteries in this country are public rather than private chapels, since they are erected not for the convenience of a single family or of private individuals, but for all the faithful of a certain locality in which the cemetery is situated, as well as for any of the faithful who may visit it. Usually, therefore, these cemetery chapels are public oratories in the strict sense. If this is so, then they are to be regarded as proper places for the hearing of confessions.

ARTICLE 6. *Places Legitimately Destined for the Hearing of Confessions*

Confessions may lawfully be heard solely in a place legitimately destined for the hearing of confessions. A place is legitimately destined when it is lawfully designated by the competent superior.[35] Whether the place is designated habitually or merely on occasion does not matter, for according to a response of the Pontifical Commission for the Authentic Interpretation of the Code as given under date of February 12, 1935, even those places which are chosen on and for an individual occasion must in accordance with canon 910, § 1, be considered as legitimately destined for the hearing of confessions.[36] Therefore the phrase, "places legitimately destined for the hearing of confessions," stands as a genus under which come two different species, namely, "places habitually destined" and "places chosen on occasion according to canon 910, § 1."

---

34. "Aediculae in coemeterio a familiis seu personis privatis ad suam sepulturam erectae, sunt oratoria privata."

35. Goyeneche, "De Confessione Religiosarum," *Apollinaris,* VIII (1935), 557.

36. *AAS,* XXVII (1935), 92; cf. also Bouscaren, *The Canon Law Digest,* II, 161.

To designate a place which has legitimately been destined in a habitual manner for the hearing of confessions the Code uses the term "confessional seat" (*sedes confessionalis*).[37] The reason for this assertion is that, since the two phrases, "places destined habitually" and "places chosen on occasion," point to all the places in which confessions may lawfully be heard, to include them both under the term "confessional seat" would make canon 910, § 1, unintelligible, for this canon states that outside the confessional seat the confessions of women are not to be heard except in cases of infirmity or necessity. Therefore the places which are simply chosen on and for an individual occasion must be excluded from the orbit of the term "confessional seat."

In a sense, any place in which confessions are heard lawfully, whether it is destined habitually or on and for an individual occasion, may rightly be called a confessional. For according to its essence a confessional is any place which is destined for the hearing of confessions.[38] However, this is not the sense in which the term is used in law. Traditional usage has employed the word "confessional" in a much more restricted sense to mean a small wooden cell-like structure constructed according to a certain prescribed form. It was in this meaning that St. Charles Borromeo first used the term "confessional." On the inside the confessional contains a seat for the confessor, and on the outside a prie-dieu for the penitent, or, as happens more often, a prie-dieu on either side for penitents who are heard alternately. The penitent is separated from the confessor by a window-like opening which is equipped with a fixed grating minutely perforated, which arrangement enables the penitent and the confessor to hear each other's

37. Cerato stated: "Pro confessionali sede intelligi debet quaelibet sedes, quae in ecclesiis et oratoriis publicis sit constituta ex stabili destinatione ad audiendas confessiones, sive formam sedis confessionalis habeat sitque in ipsa ecclesia, sive cellula quaedam sit in sacrario posita pro surdastris, aut ibidem quoddam sessorium confessario et genuflexorium pro poenitente cum imagine crucifixi." *De Delicto Sollicitationis* (Patavii: Typis Seminarii, 1922), n. 47.

38. Rota accepted the term in this meaning, but with the result of much confusion. Cf. *Enchiridion Confessarii et Iudicis Ecclesiastici seu Ratio Compendiosa iudicandi in utroque foro de abusu sacramenti poenitentiae et oeconomice procedendi in caeteris clericorum causis disciplinaribus et criminalibus* (Augustae Taurinorum, 1884), n. 294 (hereafter cited *Enchiridion*).

voice, but at the same time precludes for them the possibility of seeing or touching each other.[39]

It is easily seen that on the score of the form in which it is constructed a confessional differs only accidentally and not essentially from other places legitimately destined to serve habitually for the hearing of confessions. The confessional and other places legitimately destined to serve habitually for the hearing of confessions are as two species under the one genus "confessional seat," which, as already explained, means any place legitimately destined in an abiding manner for the hearing of confessions. The Code, it may be noted here, nowhere speaks of the confessional as such; rather, it refers simply to the "confessional seat." In deference to traditional usage the writer has preferred to retain the word "confessional" in its restricted meaning. On the score both of its external form and of its habitual use the confessional is a place legitimately destined for the hearing of confessions. In this sense every confessional is a place legitimately destined for the hearing of confessions. But it is not true that every place which is legitimately destined for the hearing of confessions is at the same time constituted as a confessional, if one understands this term in the meaning just explained.

A. PLACES HABITUALLY DESTINED FOR THE HEARING OF CONFESSIONS

After the response which was issued by the Pontifical Commission on February 12, 1935, there can be no further doubt as to what is meant by a place legitimately destined for the hearing of confessions. Prior to that time, however, the authors were not in agreement on the meaning of that phrase. Some,[40] to whose opinion Coronata attaches the weight of greater probability,[41] taught that the confessional is a small structure built according to a prescribed form and generally placed in a church, and that on the other hand the places which in addition to the confessional strictly so called are destined habitually for the hearing of

39. Coronata, *Institutiones Iuris Canonici ad usum utriusque cleri et scholarum De Sacramentis Tractatus Canonicus* (3 vols., Taurini-Romae: Marietti, 1943-1946), I, n. 440 (hereafter cited *De Sacramentis*).

40. Cf. Cerato, *De Delicto Sollicitationis,* n. 47.

41. *De Sacramentis,* I, n. 441.

confessions are all those places which, although they do not have the same external form as the confessional, nevertheless are destined in an abiding or habitual manner for the hearing of confessions. These are as two species that fall under the genus called "confessional seat." The destined places which are not of the same external form as that of a confessional may consist simply of a seat for the confessor and a prie-dieu, equipped with a grille, for the penitent. In addition to confessionals and other places legitimately destined to serve habitually for the hearing of confessions, or, in other words, in addition to confessional seats, places chosen on and for a single occasion according to canon 910, § 1, must also be considered as legitimately destined. But since they are designated merely on and for an individual occasion they will be treated separately.

The designation of places for the hearing of confessions is to be made by the competent superior, that is, the local ordinary or the regular superior, who must give at least a tacit consent.[42] In a particular case by way of exception the superioress or the confessor may choose a place in accordance with canon 910, § 1, and the place then becomes legitimately designated by the very fact that it fulfills the requirements of the law.[43] As long as a place is legitimately designated for the hearing of confessions, all confessions which are heard therein, if the other requirements are duly met, are lawful and therefore always valid.[44]

Other authors, among whom Rota is to be numbered, stated that a confessional and a place legitimately destined for the hearing of confessions are substantially one and the same thing.[45] Rota taught:

> Confessionale est velut iudicis in foro sacramentali cathedra, et est cellula lignea iuxta cuiusque Dioecesis Synodales praescriptiones exstructa, et ordinario saltem pro mulieribus habens laminam ferream ex utraque parte ipsius cum foraminibus parvis, quaeque in ecclesia collocetur. Confessionale est locus ad audiendas confessiones

42. Anonymous, "Pontificiae Commissionis Codici Interpretando Praepositae Responsiones Authenticae," *Jus Pontificium* (Romae: 1921-1940), III (1923), 119.

43. Regatillo, *Ius Sacramentarium,* I, n. 669.

44. Goyeneche, "De Confessione Religiosarum," *Apollinaris,* VIII (1935), 557.

45. *Enchiridion,* n. 294.

legitime destinatus, sed inter loca ista legitime destinata veniunt etiam subsellia, vel loca, vel cellulae, non ad praedictam formam extructae, sed diversimode pro diversis circumstantiis, dummodo ibi ex ordinaria consuetudine, et servatis servandis, confessiones audiantur, prout in sacristia, in domibus religiosis, in conservatoriis, etc.[46]

With all this it is very easy to be in agreement. However, when Rota later identified confessionals with places legitimately destined for the hearing of confessions, he raised an altogether different issue, from which there inevitably resulted a confusion of terms. To describe a confessional by calling it a place legitimately destined for the hearing of confessions was one thing. But to mention other places destined for the hearing of confessions, as for example benches or cells not constructed according to the previously described form of a confessional, and to identify them with confessionals the while their own proper nomenclature was still retained, was to invite a confusion in terminology. It is readily conceded that this discussion involves only accidental and not essential points. However, at any rate, clarity of expression is greatly desired.

In addition to calling upon the authority of D'Annibale (1815-1892), with whom he agreed, Rota offered two other reasons why he considered a confessional and a place legitimately destined for the hearing of confessions to be substantially the same. The first of these reasons he derived from the very nature of a confessional. According to Rota, a confessional is a place habitually destined for the hearing of confessions, destined both because of its form and because of its habitual use as a place for the hearing of confessions:

Confessionale est locus ad confessiones destinatus. Dicitur autem destinatus cumulative, tum ob formam, quam praefert, tum ob habitualem usum ibidem excipiendi confessiones.[47]

But in another place he stated:

Confessionale est velut genus, et loca destinata sicut et loca electa ad confessiones (nam et ista, dum ibi fit confessio, sunt vera confessionalia) sunt quasi species eiusdem.[48]

46. *Enchiridion*, n. 293.
47. *Enchiridion*, n. 294.
48. *Enchiridion*, n. 295.

Does not this statement contradict his own definition of a confessional as a place habitually destined for the hearing of confessions? In order to be consistent, then, would he not have had to say that a confessional is a place destined or chosen for the hearing of confessions? And if he had said that, should he not also have said that a confessional is any place in which confessions are legitimately heard? Rota's readiness to invoke manifold distinctions for the terms which he used seems to have brought confusion rather than a clarification.

Next to be considered is Rota's second argument. Formisano, Bishop of Nola, sought a response from the Sacred Congregation of the Holy Office in 1874 on the meaning of "confessional" and "places destined for the hearing of confessions."[49] He asked if the places in which the confessions of nuns are usually heard are to be considered as places destined for the hearing of confessions, or, in other words, as true confessionals. The Sacred Congregation of the Holy Office replied in the affirmative.[50]

Rota's opinion that the question which Bishop Formisano proposed to the Sacred Congregation set down "places destined for the hearing of confessions" in opposition to "true confessionals" does not seem warranted. For the latter of these two phrases must be accepted as being in apposition to the former in order to retain the meaning expressed by Formisano himself:

> Sempre che sono stato interrogato sopra di questa circostanza ho risposto, sembrarmi, salvo sempre il giudizio di persone più competenti in tali materie, che somiglianti luoghi [destinati] si dovevano riputare come veri e proprii confessionali, sì perchè tali luoghi sono i confessionali delle claustrali, e delle altre donne chiuse nei conservatorii, o ritiri ecc. sì perchè come tali sono da tutti riputati, sì ancora perchè la forma dei confessionali è accessoria, varia, e soggetta a cambiamenti.[51]

Obviously Formisano regarded such places destined for the hearing of confessions as true confessionals.

---

49. Cf. *Commentario sulla Costituzione Apostolicae Sedis* (6. ed., Napoli, 1876), pp. 95-96 (hereafter cited *Commentario*).

50. S. C. S. Off., 25 nov. 1874 — *Fontes*, n. 1033.

51. *Commentario*, p. 96.

Furthermore, when the Sacred Congregation of the Holy Office replied in the affirmative, Rota accepted this to be a general affirmation that all places destined for the hearing of confessions are true confessionals. However, this seems an unwarranted extension of the response of the Sacred Congregation. For the Sacred Congregation in its reply used the words *prout proponitur*. Therefore, in this particular case it is true that they were to be regarded as one and the same thing, but not in all cases. Thus in religious houses the little cells, e. g. in the sacristy, which were constructed according to the form of the ordinary confessional were to be considered as confessionals.[52] They were true confessionals and also places habitually destined for the hearing of confessions. However, they were true confessionals not for the reason that they were places destined for the hearing of confessions, but for the reason that they were constructed according to the form of true confessionals. The present writer readily admits that they could rightly be called confessionals whenever they were constructed according to the form of a confessional. But if they were not so constructed, then they should simply have been called confessional seats or places habitually destined for the hearing of confessions.

B. PLACES INDIVIDUALLY CHOSEN FOR THE HEARING OF CONFESSIONS

A place chosen on and for a single occasion for the hearing of confessions may be described negatively as one which is not designated for the habitual hearing of confessions. More exactly, however, it may be considered positively as a place which under exceptional circumstances is chosen for the hearing of a single confession or even of many confessions on some individual occasion. The essential requirement is that it be selected by way of individual choice (*per modum actus*), that is, for as long a time as there continues the particular necessity which requires the choosing or selecting of such a place. The choice must be made according to the norm of canon 910, § 1. It may be, for example, a place which along the highway is chosen for the

52. Giraldi, *Expositio Iuris Pontificii iuxta recentiorem ecclesiae disciplinam in duas partes distributa* (2 vols., Romae, 1769), II, 639.

hearing of a particular traveler's confession, or it may be a place which in the church is chosen on the occasion of a mission for the hearing of many penitents over a period of one or two weeks. Once the place has been chosen in accordance with canon 910, § 1, it becomes *ipso facto* legitimately designated by the law itself.

The choice of such a place may be made by the legitimate superior, by the confessor, or even by the penitent. For example, the pastor on the occasion of a mission, or a superior or superioress at the time of a general retreat for an entire religious community, may make the choice. More frequently, perhaps, it will actually be made by the confessor himself. Only less often will there be need or reason for the penitent to choose the place. In all cases, however, there must be a good reason. Though it need not be a grave reason, it must always furnish a genuine cause. By way of example, such reasons may be the lack of a sufficient number of legitimately designated confessional seats to receive all the penitents during a general convention, a pilgrimage, or a mission. It may also be that the penitent is offered a better opportunity of going to confession here and now. In all cases the prescription of canon 910, § 1, must be observed.

It should be said in conclusion that if a place is lawfully designated for the hearing of confessions it is lawfully destined, whether it is a confessional, a place destined habitually, or a place chosen on and for an individual occasion, according to the norm of canon 910, § 1. Accordingly, then, all confessions heard in such a place are heard lawfully.

CHAPTER IV

THE CONFESSIONS OF LAY PEOPLE

ARTICLE 1. *The Confessions of Women*

A. ORDINARY CIRCUMSTANCES

Canon 909 states that for the hearing of women's confessions a confessional seat (*sedes confessionalis*) is always to be located in an open and conspicuous place, and generally in a church, or in a public oratory, or also in a semi-public oratory which women are free to frequent. Furthermore, it should be equipped with a fixed grating perforated with small openings. The prescriptions of this canon are concerned with the proximate place for the hearing of confessions as distinguished from the remote place which is mentioned in canon 908. Thus a confessor may not lawfully hear the confessions of women simply for the reason that they approach him in a church, or in a public or semi-public oratory. Under ordinary circumstances that satisfies only half the law. For the law further requires that a properly equipped confessional seat be used.

The church or oratory in which such a confessional seat is placed must be designated as a place in which women's confessions may habitually be heard. If a place is approved merely for the hearing of men's confessions, it does not satisfy the prescription of this canon. The confessions of women are not legitimately heard in such a place.

Furthermore, if a place is approved for the hearing of one particular woman's confession, one may raise the question whether the confessions of other women may lawfully be heard therein. The reason for this is that by the use of the word "women" (*mulieribus*) the canon indicates that women in general must be free to frequent the oratory. However, it must be answered that if the requirements of the Code for hearing the confession of one woman are sufficiently fulfilled, they necessarily suffice for the hearing of the confessions of women in general.

The first part of canon 909, § 1, states that the confessional seat which serves the hearing of women's confessions is always to be located in an open and conspicuous place. Throughout the centuries of legislation regarding the place for the hearing of women's confessions, it will be recalled, the fact that the place be open to ready observation and general notice was consistently stressed. Even if women's confessions are heard outside their proper place in a church, or in a public or semi-public oratory, they must always be heard in an open place as much as circumstances will allow. Only grave and urgent necessity excuses from the observance of this prerequirement.

By general acceptation an open and conspicuous place is one that lends itself to easy and ready observation on the part of the faithful. It is not required that there be present anyone who actually calls into use this available act of observation. It is sufficient that the confessor and the penitent can be readily observed by the bystanders. The law is sufficiently satisfied if either the penitent or the confessor can be observed, although ordinarily it is to be preferred that both be observable to the public view. The use of curtains on the outside of the confessional is not precluded. Even if from their use it results that *de facto* neither the penitent nor the confessor can in person be seen, there is no objection provided that the confessional or confessional seat is located in an open and conspicuous place. In all cases a sufficient regard must be had for the secrecy of the confession, so that the confessional seat will not be placed so close to bystanders as to enable them to overhear the confession.

In the second part of canon 909, § 1, there is enacted the law that women's confessions are generally to be heard in a church, or in a public or semi-public oratory. The precise meaning of the word "generally" (*generatim*) must be determined according to the text and context of the particular canon in which it is found,[1] for it is susceptible of various shades of meaning.[2] All the following terms adequately express the meaning of the word in this particular canon: 1) generally; 2) in general; 3) as a rule; 4) in the greater number of cases, but not in all cases; 5) for the most part; 6) more often than not.

Inasmuch as the norm in the latter part of canon 909, § 1, obtains only generally or as a rule, it is susceptible of exceptions. Deviations from this general requirement, however, are allowable only for a just

1. Cf. canon 18.

2. Cf., e. g., canon 1708, 2°, where it means "in a general way" in contradistinction to "in a specific way."

reason, and never in consequence of a purely whimsical or arbitrary motivation. The law itself in canon 910 makes provision for exceptions. Ordinarily the local ordinary designates the place for the hearing of confessions. However, in a particular case by way of exception the superioress or the confessor may choose for a just reason any place as a place for the hearing of confessions, e. g., a parlor, a corridor, or the sacristy, provided that the other prescriptions concerning the openness of the place and the presence of a screen are also observed.[3] When the superioress or the confessor chooses the place according to canon 910, § 1, the legitimate designation comes from the law itself.

The confessional seat or confessional is to be equipped with some sort of fixed screen perforated with small openings. It is not important whether the screen is actually made of metal or of reed, as long as it is fixed and immovable, so that it cannot be opened as a window or a little door. One need not be scrupulous about the exact size of the openings. Regatillo says that they should be round and not oblong, in order to preclude the passing of any note through the screen.[4] According to a decree of the Sacred Congregation of Bishops and Regulars under date of September 22, 1645, the openings should be small enough to prevent the passage of one's little finger.[5] By the law of the Code the use of a curtain over the screen is not required. In this matter local custom and synodal legislation are to be followed, for the Code does not concern itself with this or similar minute details.

The obligation enacted in the Code, namely that a fixed barrier separate the penitent from the confessor, is a grave one.[6] Before any exception can be made there must be a proportionately grave reason. But even when an exception is made, whatever precautions are judged opportune by the local ordinary must be observed. These safeguards will offset any moral dangers that may be present when the use of the screen is dispensed with. If the ordinary has not made any prescriptions, then the demands of natural decency and propriety will constitute the guiding norms.

---

3. Regatillo, *Ius Sacramentarium,* I, n. 669.
4. *Ius Sacramentarium,* I, n. 670.
5. S. C. Ep. et Reg., *Pisauren.,* 22 sept. 1645 — *Fontes,* n. 1774.
6. Vermeersch-Creusen, *Epitome,* II, n. 197.

With reference to the confessional and its various appurtenances, Regatillo makes the practical suggestion that its construction should be such as to allow the confessor to remain comfortable with a view to safeguarding his health and to maintaining a mental alertness. A priest who has to hear confessions for long periods of time should not be exposed to unnecessary discomfort or avoidable physical fatigue through any ill-chosen method in the construction of the confessional. Every serviceable means, short of course of all luxury, can be lawfully employed for guarding the confessor's physical comfort and ease.[7]

B. EXTRAORDINARY CIRCUMSTANCES

Canon 910, § 1, makes due allowance for the exceptional circumstances which may make it necessary to hear the confessions of women outside the ordinary legitimately designated place, namely the confessional seat.[8] It is to be noted that this canon refers to all women alike, whether they be lay or religious, and whether they be growing children or grown adults.[9] Even if a confessor feels that in a particular case there is no danger in hearing a woman's confession outside the confessional seat, that is not a sufficient reason to allow him to do so, for according to canon 21 the Church's enacted laws which seek to preclude a general danger bind even if in a particular case the danger is not present.[10] The reasons that justify the legitimate exception of hearing the confessions of women outside the confessional seat are restricted to two, infirmity and any true necessity.

1) *Infirmity*

a) On the part of the penitent

The term "infirmity" includes not only what is generally and commonly called illness but also deafness and physical decrepitude because

7. *Ius Sacramentarium,* I, n. 670.

8. "Feminarum confessiones extra sedem confessionalem ne audiantur, nisi ex causa infirmitatis aliave verae necessitatis et adhibitis cautelis quas Ordinarius loci opportunas iudicaverit."

9. Cappello, *De Poenitentia,* II, n. 942.

10. "Leges latae ad praecavendum periculum generale, urgent etiamsi in casu peculiari periculum non adsit."

of old age. The Code does not specify any particular degree of gravity in the illness which will warrant the hearing of a woman's confession outside the confessional seat. Accordingly any genuine illness suffices for the emergence of an exceptional procedure in a given case. It is not required that the penitent be actually confined to bed, or that she be under the care of a physician. If the woman is sufficiently ill to need the services of a physician, then there can be no doubt of the presence of a sufficient reason for hearing her confession outside the confessional seat. By universal acceptation the sickbed of a person confined by illness, or also the room itself, must then be regarded as a place legitimately destined for the hearing of that person's confession.[11] This exemplifies the case in which the lawful designation of the place may be said to derive from the force of a custom which is in full accord with the law.

The confessor is not expected to conduct a lengthy investigation to determine the precise gravity of the penitent's illness. Yet he must be able to judge prudently and satisfactorily that the penitent is really ill. Ordinarily the confessor is able to determine this easily because of the evident circumstances in which a sick person is found. In cases of doubt the penitent is to be favored. The confessor need never be unduly anxious as long as he uses whatever precautions are prescribed by the local ordinary for those cases in which the confessions of women are heard outside the confessional seat.

Physical illness is not the only type of illness to be considered as warranting an exception. Due regard must also be had for mental or psychological illness. For example, if a woman has a strong psychological dread of the darkness of the confessional or if she suffers from claustrophobia, that is sufficient reason to hear her confession outside the confessional seat. Such a phobia, however, must not simply be alleged; it must really and truly be present. The confessor must satisfy himself in this regard before he may legitimately undertake to hear such a woman's confession outside the confessional seat. Yet he is perfectly justified in following the rule: *Semper credendum est poenitenti tam pro se quam contra se confitenti.*

---

11. Cappello, *De Poenitentia,* II, n. 684.

As regards penitents who are deaf, it is not unlikely that in the larger churches a hearing aid has been installed for the convenience of the deaf in at least one of the confessionals. Where this has not been done, it is feasible to have in the sacristy a special confessional which is designated as a place for the hearing of the confessions of the deaf. Ordinarily the sacristy is not to be considered as a place for the hearing of confessions except in cases of necessity.[12]

The II Plenary Council of Baltimore (1866) decreed that confessionals for the hearing of women's confessions were to be erected in churches, and then further explained that the sacristy was not included under the name of church. Therefore the sacristy was not to be used as a place for the hearing of confessions unless it was "a public and open place."[13]

Cappello[14] and Coronata[15] say that the sacristy may be used as a place for the hearing of the confessions of those who are deaf. If there is no confessional in the sacristy, then the confessions of women who are deaf may be heard in any fitting place and under the same conditions as in any true necessity.

Although the authors do not mention what is to be done if it is the confessor himself who is deaf, it seems perfectly logical to allow the same exception as in the case in which the penitent is deaf.

b) On the part of the confessor

The Code does not specify whether it is infirmity on the part of the confessor or on the part of the penitent that warrants an exception to the general rule that calls for the hearing of confessions in the confessional seat. It cannot rightly be argued that the Code obviously intends to refer only to the penitent. In the sources cited in the footnote to canon 910, § 1, there is none which excludes infirmity on the part of the confessor as a reason for hearing the confessions of women outside the confessional seat. Therefore it does not appear contrary to the meaning of this canon to say that infirmity or illness on the part of the

12. S. C. Ep. et Reg., *Pisauren.*, 22 sept. 1645 — *Fontes*, n. 1774.
13. *Acta*, n. 296.
14. *De Poenitentia*, II, n. 684.
15. *De Sacramentis*, I, n. 463.

confessor is likewise constituted as a sufficient reason that will allow him to hear a woman's confession outside the confessional seat. Some authors, however, defend the opposite view.[16]

The II Plenary Council of Baltimore (1866) explicitly allowed aged or infirm priests to hear the confessions of women outside the confessional seat:

> Vehementer hortamur praesules, ut omni studio curent confessionalia erigenda in omnibus ecclesiis publicis harum provinciarum: et, cum erecta fuerint, nemini sacerdotum licebit confessiones mulierum alio in loco excipere, sine speciali Ordinarii licentia. Hanc vero nunquam concedendum confidimus, praeterquam sacerdotibus aetate provectis, vel infirmis, vel ob poenitentes surdas; vel aliis in casibus, in quibus ex huius regulae observantia gravia orirentur incommoda.[17]

2) *Necessity*

As in the case of infirmity and illness, whenever the confessor out of necessity hears the confession of one or many women outside the ordinary place which is habitually designated for their confessions, he does so in a place which is chosen for the specific occasion. That is evident, for if the place were one that is habitually destined for the hearing of confessions, it could not be said that the priest hears the confession *extra sedem confessionalem.* It would not constitute an exception to the general rule enacted in canon 910, § 1. Because of the circumstances under which the confession is heard, it will often be necessary that the confession be made face to face, minus the benefit of a screen interposed between the confessor and the penitent. Authors consider the obligation of having a screen to be a grave one. Except in cases of necessity or infirmity, it is gravely illicit for a confessor to hear the confessions of women habitually or frequently when a screen is not employed.[18]

---

16. Cf. Jombart, *Dictionnaire de Droit Canonique* (Paris: Librairie Letouzey et Ané, 1924-), Fascicle XIX (1944), 66, s. v. *Confessional* (hereafter cited *Dictionnaire*).

17. *Acta,* n. 295.

18. Regatillo, *Ius Sacramentarium,* I, n. 671; Cappello, *De Poenitentia,* II, n. 942; Vermeersch-Creusen, *Epitome,* II, n. 197.

The law which requires the use of a confessional screen is a law of greater importance than the law which regulates the factor of place.[19] As long as a confessor uses a screen, even though he does not hear a woman's confession in an open place, he seems not to commit a mortal sin in the absence of any and all scandal; and sometimes his action may be free of the stigma of any kind of sin.[20]

The Code is satisfied to require a true or genuine necessity as a sufficient reason for the hearing of a woman's confession outside the confessional seat. Whatever precautions the local ordinary has prescribed for such cases must always be observed. If there are no such regulations, the ordinary rules of Christian decency and propriety must be observed. In the abstract it is not difficult to state what constitutes a true or genuine necessity. In the concrete, however, it is most difficult to explain exactly when such a necessity is verified. It is precisely for this reason that the Code does not specify the nature of a true necessity, for the close specification of limitations would defeat the purpose of the law. Ultimately the decision as to what constitutes a true necessity rests with the prudent judgment of the confessor. The choice of the place, however, may be made by the legitimate superior, the confessor, or even the penitent.

It is impossible to enumerate every kind of true necessity which is to be considered a sufficient reason that allows the confessor to hear the confessions of women outside the confessional seat. However, it will be helpful to furnish some examples.

First of all, it must be noted that the mere request of a woman to go to confession is not to be judged in itself a sufficient reason for hearing her confession outside the confessional seat. Such a practice would obviously contravene the law, and make it entirely useless and inoperative. The request of a penitent to have her confession heard will generally suffice to point to the necessity of hearing her confession, but inherently it certainly does not point to the necessity of hearing her confession outside the confessional seat. The judgment in regard to this point must be based on other grounds.

---

19. Regatillo, *Ius Sacramentarium*, I, n. 671.

20. Vermeersch-Creusen, *Epitome*, II, n. 197; Cappello, *De Poenitentia*, II, 942.

If a penitent would run the risk of a loss of her reputation by going to confession in a confessional seat, then there would be constituted a true necessity, so that the confessor would act legitimately in hearing her confession outside the confessional seat.[21] It is useless to try to determine all the particular circumstances which may have led to such a situation. Whatever the reasons may be, as long as the danger of a loss of reputation is verified, there is a true necessity.

Jombart states that if a penitent would otherwise be deprived of the opportunity of going to confession for a whole year, then there would be present a true necessity in warrant of the exceptional manner in the administration of the sacrament of penance to her.[22] However, this doctrine seems too arbitrary to allow its reduction to practice. Rather, it seems that a solution of the problem in such a case cannot abstract from the particular temperament and devotional habits of the penitent as involving the real determining factor that underlies the ultimate judgment. For example, a penitent who is accustomed to receive Holy Communion on the First Friday of every month may find herself in such circumstances that, unless she goes to confession here and now outside the confessional seat by availing herself of the opportunity of the confessor's presence, she will be deprived of the opportunity of receiving the rich benefits promised by Our Blessed Lord to those who receive Holy Communion on the first Friday of nine consecutive months. Such a necessity certainly seems to warrant the making of an exception. In general, then, if the observance of the law that calls for the hearing of a woman's confession only in the confessional seat would result in the penitent's being unable to go to confession with her usual frequency, such a situation appears to offer a sufficient reason for the making of an exception.[23]

The opportunity for a woman of going to confession here and now in order that she may receive Holy Communion at a Mass which is

21. Cf. Jombart, *Dictionnaire,* Fascicle XIX (1944), 66, s. v. *Confessional.*

22. *Loc. cit.*

23. Anonymous, "Confessions of Women outside the Confessional" (*The American Ecclesiastical Review,* Vols. I-XXXII, Philadelphia, 1889-1905; *The Ecclesiastical Review,* Vols. XXXIII-CIX, Philadelphia, 1905-1943; *The American Ecclesiastical Review,* Washington, D. C., Vol. CX, 1944-), XC (1934), 160 (hereafter cited as *AER* or *ER respectively*).

going to be celebrated immediately in that place also furnishes a sufficient reason for hearing that woman's confession outside the confessional seat.[24] If a priest, for example, has received permission from the local ordinary, in virtue of the faculty possessed by the latter by reason of the law as enacted in canon 822, § 4, to celebrate Mass in the home of a person who is sick, it may happen that someone who is in the house of the sick person requests that her confession be heard in order that she may receive Holy Communion at the Mass that is to be celebrated. The Sacred Congregation of the Sacraments on July 29, 1927, issued to the Bishop of Mondovì in Piedmont a response which involved this precise point. This Sacred Congregation replied that the faithful in these mountain hamlets could receive Holy Communion and the sacrament of confession whenever Holy Communion was brought to the sick. As regards confession, the prescriptions of canons 909 and 910 were to be observed.[25] Under such circumstances it is very often, if not always, necessary to hear confessions outside the confessional seat simply for the reason that none is available. The principal consideration in such cases concerns the use of the safeguards prescribed by the local ordinary.

Scholium. The safeguards prescribed by the local ordinary

When the confession of a woman is heard outside the confessional seat in consequence of the attendant factor of necessity or infirmity, the confessor is obliged by canon 910, § 1, to use whatever precautions are prescribed for such cases by the local ordinary. The purpose of the law in this regard is eminently reasonable and readily apparent. Because of the delicate nature of the matter which is treated in confession, and in view also of the obvious frailties of human nature, it is the intention of the Church to protect both the confessor and the penitent. Yet also constantly mindful of the axiom *sacramenta propter homines,* the Church does not desire to impose regulations which would be so difficult to observe that the faithful would repeatedly be deprived of the reception of the sacrament of penance simply for the lack of observance of these regulations.

---

24. Regatillo, *Ius Sacramentarium,* I, n. 669.
25. Bouscaren, *The Canon Law Digest,* I, 391.

The Code imposes the general obligation to observe the precautions prescribed by the local ordinary, but entrusts to particular legislation the task of defining specifically all the details.[26] Therefore much rests upon the prudent judgment of the ordinary, and he will necessarily be guided by the circumstances of the particular place. From the decrees of the Sacred Congregation for the Propagation of the Faith and of the Sacred Congregation of Bishops and Regulars, as well as from particular synodal and conciliar legislation prior to the Code, a typical list of such safeguards may be compiled.

If the woman's confession is heard outside the confessional seat but nevertheless still in the church, the local ordinary could prescribe that the confession be heard in a very prominent place, for example, at the altar rail. Thus the confessor would sit inside the sanctuary and the woman would kneel outside the sanctuary on the altar step.[27] The ordinary could require that the place be well-lighted, or that there be present in the church at least a third person who can act as a witness.[28] Furthermore, he could demand that the confessor shield his face with the sleeve of his cassock or his surplice, if he wears one;[29] that the women veil their faces;[30] that there be a veil or cloth between the penitent and the confessor.[31] These safeguards are not all to be recommended with equal vigor. Some of them would be highly impractical in this country, as for example that of requiring women to veil their face, since it is not a common practice among women here to wear veils. The ordinary may also require that, when from necessity a screen cannot be used, then some kind of barrier, for example the altar rail, is to separate the penitent from the confessor.

In those cases in which a woman's confession is heard in a private home, it would be eminently wise and reasonable to require that the

---

26. Romani, *Institutiones Iuris Canonici* (2 vols. in 3, Vol. II, *Ius Administrativum de Sacramentis,* Pars Prior, Romae: Editrice "Iustitia," 1944), II, Pars Prior, n. 377.

27. Cf. Synod of Paris (1198), Cap. VI, n. 2 — Mansi, XXII, 678.

28. Cf. Synod of Cologne (1280), Cap. VIII — Mansi, XXIV, 353.

29. Cf. Provincial Council of Avignon (1725), Cap. III — Mansi, XXXVII, 324-5.

30. Cf. S. C. de Prop. Fide (C. P. pro Sin.—Chan-si), 17 mart. 1785 — *Fontes,* n. 4600.

31. Regatillo, *Ius Sacramentarium,* I, n. 671.

door of the room be left open.[32] Thus the confessor and the penitent will remain in full view to whatever persons may be present in the house. However, the necessity of guaranteeing the secrecy of the confession may sometimes make this inadvisable.

If the local ordinary has not prescribed any safeguards, the confessor is obliged to use whatever precautions are demanded by natural decency and propriety.

ARTICLE 2. *The Confessions of Men*

Canon 909, § 1, enacts a universal law concerning the place for the hearing of women's confessions. From this fact some authors[33] believed that the following paragraph in the same canon, which requires the confessional seat to be equipped with a fixed grille having minutely perforated openings, also applies only to women.[34] However, others argued that canon 909, § 2, refers to the confessional seat for all penitents alike.[35] Because of this doubt, the Pontifical Commission was asked:

> Whether canon 909, § 2: "The confessional seat shall be provided with a fixed screen with small perforations between the penitent and the confessor," is to be observed in the confessions of women only: or whether it is to be generally observed for penitents as the proper way of hearing confessions in churches and public oratories.[36]

---

32. Cf. S. C. de Prop. Fide (C. G. — Hiberniae), 12 febr. 1821 — *Fontes*, n. 4723.

33. Sartori, *Enchiridion Canonicum seu Sanctae Sedis Responsiones post Editum Codicem I. C. Datae iuxta Canonum Codicis Ordinem Digestae Notulisque Ordinatae* (8. ed., Romae: Pontificium Athenaeum Antonianum, 1947), p. 179 (hereafter cited *Enchiridion*).

34. "Sedes confessionalis crate fixa ac tenuiter perforata inter poenitentem et confessarium sit instructa."

35. Anonymous, "Pontificiae Commissionis Codici Interpretando Praepositae Responsiones Authenticae," *Jus Pontificium*, III (1923), 121.

36. *AAS*, XII (1920), 576; cf. also Bouscaren, *The Canon Law Digest*, I, 417. Translation by the writer.

It replied under date of November 24, 1920:

> In the negative to the first part; in the affirmative to the second; without prejudice, however, to the provisions of canon 910, § 2.[37]

In this response, which seems to give a more extensive meaning to canon 909, § 1,[38] there is now such clarity that there can no longer be any doubt. This response is perfectly reasonable if canons 908-910 are taken as a unit and not as isolated canons. For the legislator seems to have arranged these canons so that canon 908 enunciates a general principle concerning the confessional seat; canon 909 accurately describes the ordinary confessional seat for both sexes; and canon 910 treats of the extraordinary confessional seat for men and women.[39]

According to the response of November 24, 1920, whenever the confessions of men are heard in a church or in public or semi-public oratory, then as a rule there must be used a confessional seat which is equipped with a screen. But this does not appear to be a grave requirement, and therefore any good reason may be regarded as furnishing an excuse from the law.[40] Thus for the confessions of men there may be used, as distinct from the confessional seat used for women, a simple prie-dieu and a seat. If the confessional seats in a church are equipped with a fixed screen, then they sufficiently satisfy the prescriptions of the Code and the response of the Pontifical Commission as given on November 24, 1920, so that the confessions of both men and women may be heard there.[41]

Canon 910, § 2, from whose prescriptions the response of the Pontifical Commission does not derogate, states that it is permitted to hear the confessions of men even in private homes.[42] Cappello remarks that what is here said about private homes must also be said *a pari*, if not *a fortiori*, about domestic or private oratories. Any good reason is sufficient to permit the hearing of the confessions of men in private

---

37. *Loc. cit.*

38. Sartori, *Enchiridion*, p. 179.

39. Anonymous, "Pontificiae Commissionis Codici Interpretando Praepositae Responsiones Authenticae," *Jus Pontificium*, III (1923), 121.

40. Vermeersch-Creusen, *Epitome*, II, n. 197.

41. Coronata, *De Sacramentis*, I, n. 464.

42. "Confessiones virorum etiam in aedibus privatis excipere licet."

homes. Naturally the emergence of scandal must always be precluded, and the norms of prudence and modesty must be duly observed.[43]

If a place is fitting for the hearing of confessions, the confessions of men may be heard therein. And since any good reason is sufficient to hear the confessions of men outside the confessional seat, it will never be gravely unlawful to hear them outside the confessional seat. One should always observe the particular customs of the place.

Regatillo says that the response of November 24, 1920, as given by the Pontifical Commission, does not abrogate the immemorial custom existing in Spain and Spanish America, and possibly also in other places, by which the confessions of men are heard apart from the use of a grille interposed between the confessor and the penitent.[44] He adds, however, that the Holy See has manifested its desire to the Spanish bishops that they introduce gradually the use of the screen as much as possible. When the confessions of men are heard outside the confessional seat, the special safeguards prescribed by the local ordinary for the confessions of women need not be observed.[45]

ARTICLE 3. *The Confessional Seat Required for Validity?*

The Code does not require churches to have a confessional strictly so called, but is satisfied simply to demand a properly equipped and properly located confessional seat. The II Plenary Council of Baltimore (1866) urged all the prelates to see to it that confessionals were erected in all public churches.[46] Though the Council then urged more than the Code requires now in this matter, it is not contrary to the latter. It should be recalled, however, that the Council did not impose any strict obligation; rather, it made a strong recommendation. Therefore it still remains in force as a strong recommendation.

It may be asked if the confessional or the confessional seat is required for the validity of the confessions of lay women. This question in regard to the confessions of women religious will be considered

---

43. *De Poenitentia,* II, n. 942, 5°.
44. *Ius Sacramentarium,* I, n. 672.
45. Romani, *Institutiones Iuris Canonici,* II, Pars Prior, n. 377.
46. *Acta,* nn. 295-296.

later. As regards the confessions of men, it is certain that the element of place never affects the validity.

Although the obligation imposed by canon 909 is indeed a grave one with regard to the confessions of women, before one may conclude that its requirements must be met in order that the confessions of women may be valid, it is necessary that these prescriptions be enacted in such a way as to indicate either expressly or in some equivalent manner that any contravention of the law entails invalidity as its juridical effect.[47] As long as this is not clearly indicated by the canon, one may safely conclude that an act, even though performed contrary to the requirements of the law, is not invalid. Canon 909, therefore, is entirely concerned with the requirements for the lawful, and not also for the valid, procedure.[48]

47. Cf. canon 11.

48. Anonymous, "Is [a] Confessional Required for Valid Confession of Women?" *ER*, CII (1940), 532-533.

CHAPTER V

THE PLACE FOR THE HEARING OF THE CONFESSIONS OF RELIGIOUS

ARTICLE 1. *The Confessions of Women Religious*

A. THE OCCASIONAL CONFESSION

Canon 522 which deals with the occasional confessor for women religious has received much attention from the canonical commentators and has been the subject of several decrees emanating from the Pontifical Commission for the Authentic Interpretation of the Code. One author has called canon 522 a *canon vexatissimus*.[1] Another writer says that it has been the subject of more written articles than perhaps any other canon in the Code.[2]

In the light of several interpretations made by the Pontifical Commission the importance of canon 522 is very great. It is clear now beyond all doubt that the element of place affects the validity of a confession made by a woman religious to an occasional confessor. In order to understand fully the relation of this particular requirement to the whole canon it is necessary first to consider the other prescriptions of this same canon. Though it is not the purpose of this work to consider in all its details the import of canon 522, nevertheless to explain but one point, namely the element of place, to the exclusion of the other conditions upon which the practical application of this canon also depends, is to leave incomplete and inadequate the knowledge of the confessor who hopes to use this canon with a feeling of confidence that he is faithfully fulfilling all its prescriptions.

Canon 522 states:

> If, notwithstanding the prescriptions of canons 520 and 521, any religious, for the peace of her conscience, has recourse to a con-

---

1. Toso, *Ad Codicem Iuris Canonici Benedicti XV Pont. Max. Auctoritate Promulgatum Commentaria Minora* (5 vols., Romae: Ius Pontificium, 1918-1927), V, 65.

2. Chelodi, *Ius Canonicum de Personis* (3. ed. curavit Pius Ciprotti, Trento: Libreria Moderna Editrice, 1942), n. 258 (hereafter cited *De Personis*).

fessor approved by the local ordinary for hearing the confessions of women, this confession, whether made in a church or in an oratory, even a semi-public oratory, is valid and lawful, every contrary privilege being revoked, and the superioress may not prohibit it or make any inquiry concerning it, even indirectly; the religious moreover are under no obligation to inform the superioress on the matter.[3]

According to Regatillo[4] there are three reasons for this canon: (1) Daily reception of Holy Communion is recommended to all the faithful, especially to religious. But women religious are often bothered by scruples and therefore would sometimes omit the reception of Holy Communion only to be embarrassed by the wonderment caused among the other members of the community. Furthermore, since a confessor approved for the hearing of their confessions is not always available, it is fitting that women religious should have access to a confessor approved for the hearing of women's confessions. (2) A similar privilege is granted to male religious by canon 519.[5] (3) Freedom of conscience is best assured if a religious, when she does not have confidence in the confessors appointed habitually for the hearing of her confession, or cannot call them, or does not desire to do so, is then able to approach an occasional confessor.

The Code extends the privilege conferred by canon 522 beyond the limits imposed by the decree *Cum de sacramentalibus,* which was issued by the Sacred Congregation for Religious under date of February 3, 1913.[6] According to this decree it was required that the religious be

3. Translation by the writer.

4. *Ius Sacramentarium,* I, n. 462.

5. "Firmis constitutionibus quae confessionem statis temporibus praecipiunt vel suadent apud determinatos confessarios peragendam, si religiosus, etiam exemptus, ad suae conscientiae quietem, confessarium adeat ab Ordinario loci approbatum, etsi inter designatos non recensitum, confessio, revocato quolibet contrario privilegio, valida et licita est; et confessarius potest religiosum absolvere etiam a peccatis et censuris in religione reservatis."

6. "Si quando moniales aut sorores extra propriam domum, quavis de causa, versari contigerit, liceat iis in qualibet ecclesia vel oratorio, etiam semi-publico, confessionem peragere apud quemvis confessarium pro utroque sexu approbatum. Antistita neque id prohibere, neque de ea re inquirere potest, ne indirecte quidem; religiosaeque nihil antistitae suae referre tenentur." — *AAS,* V (1913), 64, n. 14; *Pontes,* n. 4416.

outside her own house when she availed herself of this privilege. The Code removed this restriction by omitting the phrase *extra propriam domum* as it was contained in the aforementioned decree. Furthermore, the legislator's intention of favoring liberty of conscience is apparent, and any difficulties which are alleged in order to restrict this freedom are of secondary importance. This is readily seen from the reference to canons 520 and 521, whose prescriptions notwithstanding, a religious is still free to avail herself of the privilege granted by canon 522, and also from the revocation of any contrary privilege which could derogate from the prescriptions of canon 522.

Vermeersch (1858-1936) stated that there were some theologians and prelates who in the application of canon 522 were somewhat strict, since in their interpretation of this canon they were reluctant to approve its apparent leniency.[7] Consequently he did not think it strange if they endeavored to bring about a direct or indirect abrogation or limitation of the canon in view of their reluctance to admit innovations, or because of their fear that the granted liberty would be abused. However, so he continued, every positive law entails some inconveniences, and once the almost inevitable abuses which take place at first have subsided, there will follow a rational use of the liberty which was granted. And so it has been.

1) *Interpretation of Canon 522*

Authors were not agreed on the rule to be used in the interpretation of canon 522, that is, whether the canon should be interpreted strictly or broadly. Goyeneche, for example, said that this canon must be subjected to a strict interpretation, since it contains an exception to the general and universal law enacted in canon 876, § 1,[8] which ex-

---

7. "Moralis et Pastoralis Consideratio de Religiosarum Confessione Facta Confessario ex can. 522" —*Periodica de Religiosis et Missionariis* (Brugis, 1905-1919; *Periodica de Re Canonica et Morali utilia praesertim Religiosis et Missionariis*, Brugis, 1920-1927; *Periodica de Re Morali, Canonica, Liturgica*, Brugis, 1927-1936, et Romae, 1937-), XI (1922), (2) (hereafter cited *Periodica*).

8. "Revocata qualibet contraria particulari lege seu privilegio, sacerdotes tum saeculares tum religiosi, cuiusvis gradus aut officii, ad confessiones quarumcumque religiosarum ac novitiarum valide et licite recipiendas peculiari iurisdictione indigent, salvo praescripto can. 239, § 1, n. 1, 522, 523."

ception, according to canon 19,[9] is to be interpreted strictly.[10] But the difficulty lay in the very fact of trying to determine the strict sense of the canon. Since the conditions indistinctly set down therein were required for lawfulness and validity, its prescriptions were equivocal.

Other authors argued that canon 522 is not an exception to canon 876, § 1, since this latter canon makes explicit mention of canon 522. Therefore it is a privilege, and according to canon 68 any doubtful import in the privilege is to be interpreted broadly. Among these was Vermeersch, who argued that since canon 876, § 1, makes special mention of canon 522 not as an exception to the law but as a prescription, this same canon 876, § 1, is not a universal law in the proper sense, nor is canon 522 an exception to it.[11] This opinion seems to have intrinsic as well as extrinsic probability, and to the present writer seems more acceptable than the contrary view.

2) *The Conditions of Canon 522*

Canon 522 points without any distinction to four requirements for the valid and lawful use of this privilege: (1) the confession must be made for the peace of one's conscience; (2) the religious must "approach" the confessor; (3) the confessor must be approved for the hearing of women's confessions; and (4) the confession must be made in a church or in an oratory which has at least a semi-public status. It was doubtful whether all these conditions, especially the condition which refers to the element of place, were required both for validity and for lawfulness. Authors took various stands. Generally, the condition that the confession be made for the peace of one's conscience was considered by the authors as being required only for the lawfulness of the confession. The conditions that the religious "approach" the con-

---

9. "Leges quae poenam statuunt, aut liberum iurium exercitium coarctant, aut exceptionem a lege continent, strictae subsunt interpretationi."

10. "De vi can. 522," *Commentarium pro Religiosis* (Romae, 1920-1934; *Commentarium pro Religiosis et Missionariis,* Romae, 1935-), II (1921), 15 (hereafter cited *Commentarium*).

11. "Interpretatio can. 19 de stricta quarundam legum interpretatione, cum nonnullis applicationibus," *Periodica,* XI (1922), (14).

fessor and that the confessor be approved for the hearing of women's confessions were regarded as affecting the validity. The final condition which concerned the element of place caused the greatest discussion, for some thought that the Code intended that condition as relating to the validity of the act, while others argued that it was intended as relating simply to the lawfulness of the act of confession. Before consideration is given to the condition which deals with the element of place, it seems imperative first to explain more fully the other conditions.

When canon 522 speaks of a woman religious (*aliqua religiosa*) it uses the term in a generic sense to include all women religious without any distinction as regards solemn or simple vows, or without any reference to whether they belong to an institute of pontifical or diocesan approval.[12] However, though nuns who observe the papal cloister enjoy this privilege, they will not be able to use it frequently because of the restrictions of the cloister. As regards novices, though they are not religious in the strict sense inasmuch as they are not professed with vows, nevertheless by reason of the prescriptions of canon 566, § 1, they follow the same discipline as religious in regard to confessors and confession. Furthermore, canon 876, § 1, explicitly mentions them. Quasi-religious, that is, women living a life in common without vows, are likewise likened in law to religious in the matter of confessors and confession, and hence they share, as do the religious, in this same privilege.[13] Postulants may confess to any priest who has a general approval for hearing the confessions of the faithful. Therefore there does not arise the question of extending the same privilege to them.

a) Peace of Conscience

According to the common opinion of the authors, the condition that the confession be made for the peace of one's conscience affects only the lawfulness of the absolution given in the sacrament of penance. The very difficulty in judging a matter so purely subjective sufficiently indicates that this condition is not required for validity.[14] Fanfani says that any confession which is seriously made with the in-

12. Cf. canon 488, 7°.
13. Cf. canon 675.
14. Coronata, *Institutiones*, II, n. 551, note 2.

tention of receiving absolution is by its very nature ordained for one's peace of conscience.[15]

The best judge in this matter is primarily the religious herself, and secondarily the confessor whom she has chosen. This requirement is set not as a *conditio sine qua non,* but simply as a caution for insuring the fruitful reception of the sacrament. Accordingly the requirement is verified whenever the religious seeks absolution for the reason that she considers it as serving her spiritual welfare or greater progress in the spiritual life, or simply out of devotion on the occasion of some great feast, even though she is not harassed with scruples, bothered with doubts, worried with temptations, or burdened with any grave sin. If the law required more than this right disposition on the part of the religious, it would almost inevitably serve as an occasion for increased scruples and anxieties. This undesirable result obviously is not what is intended by the legislator.

b) The Approach

After the promulgation of the Code there was a controversy among canonists concerning the meaning of the word *adeat* in canon 522. It was disputed whether this word should be interpreted broadly to mean that a religious not only could go to the confessor but also could call him to come to her expressly to hear her confession. It is needless now to consider the details of the controversy, since the matter was settled definitively through an authentic response of the Pontifical Commission under date of December 28, 1927. It replied in the negative to the following question:

> Whether the word *adeat* of canon 522 is so to be understood that the confessor cannot be called by the religious herself to a place which is legitimately destined for the confessions of women or of women religious.[16]

15. *De Iure Religiosorum ad Normam Codicis Iuris Canonici* (ed. altera, Taurini-Romae: Ex Officina Libraria Marietti, 1925), n. 127 (hereafter cited *De Iure Religiosorum*).

16. *AAS,* XX (1927), 61, II; cf. also Bouscaren, *The Canon Law Digest,* I, 296. Translation by the writer.

Thus the condition here set now imports either of two things: (1) a religious who desires to make a sacramental confession may use any legitimate occasion in order to approach a confessor who is approved by the local ordinary for the hearing of women's confessions, and (2) she may also for the same purpose call such a confessor to the convent or to the place where she actually is living. However, she may use only those means that are permitted to her, that is, she may not leave the convent without permission, nor may she violate the regimen of the house. The superioress is not obliged to call the confessor, nor may the religious demand that she be given such an opportunity.[17]

The condition imposed by the word *adeat* is one that relates to the factor of validity for the absolution. It is the common opinion among the authors that the absolution is invalid if it is given by a confessor who is not approved for hearing the confessions of women religious, but who on his own initiative and with a misplaced reliance on canon 522 has gone to their oratory to hear the confession of a religious.[18]

c) A Confessor Approved for the Confessions of Women

In the decree *Cum de sacramentalibus* of February 3, 1913, the Sacred Congregation for Religious required in this matter that the confessor have received approval for hearing the confessions of both men and women. Canon 522 simply demands that he have received the approval of the local ordinary for hearing the confessions of women. Inasmuch as the Code uses the plural form (*mulieribus*) it would not suffice if the confessor had received jurisdiction to hear the confession of only one woman.[19] A confessor who has jurisdiction simply and exclusively to hear the confessions of the nuns of a particular convent is included within the terms of this canon, for women religious are certainly included under the generic term "women." The provision, namely that the confessor have jurisdiction for the hearing of women's

17. Cf. the private response of the Sacred Congregation for Religious given on December 1, 1921, as reported in Bouscaren, *The Canon Law Digest*, I, 296-297.

18. Schaefer, *De Religiosis ad Normam Codicis Iuris Canonici* (3. ed., Romae: Typis Polyglottis Vaticanis, 1940), n. 176 (hereafter cited *De Religiosis*).

19. Vermeersch-Creusen, *Epitome*, I, n. 644.

confessions, is incorporated in canon 522 in view of the practice in some localities of limiting younger priests to the hearing of men's confessions only. In this country this condition offers no difficulty, for all confessors everywhere receive jurisdiction over the faithful of both sexes in the authorization to hear confessions.[20]

d) The Place

It remains now to consider the requirement of canon 522 concerning the place for the hearing of confessions of women religious when these make their confession to an occasional confessor. The fourth condition postulated in this canon points to the fact that the confessions be made in a church or in an oratory which has at least a semi-public status. Authors doubted whether the element of place thus postulated was required for the validity as well as the lawfulness of the absolution. A reply of the Pontifical Commission given under date of November 24, 1920, failed to settle the doubts. The Commission was asked:

> Whether the words of canon 522: "confessio in qualibet ecclesia vel oratorio etiam semi-publico peracta, valida et licita est," are to be understood in the sense that a confession outside those places is not only unlawful but also invalid.

It replied:

> Canon 522 is to be understood in the sense that the confessions which religious make for their peace of conscience to a confessor approved by the ordinary of the place for the confessions of women are lawful and valid, provided that they are made in a church or in an oratory, even a semi-public one, or in a place which is legitimately destined for the confessions of women.[21]

It appears that the Pontifical Commission did not desire to answer directly the doubt as it was proposed, but rather preferred to emphasize the positive import of canon 522, namely the liberty of conscience. However, in this response which stated that such confessions are lawful

---

20. Cf. Snee and Clark, *Diocesan Faculties in the United States* (Woodstock: Woodstock College Press, 1948), nn. 125-130.

21. *AAS,* XII (1920), 575; cf. also Bouscaren, *The Canon Law Digest,* I, 295. Translation by the writer.

and valid provided that they are made in a church or oratory, even a semi-public one, there were also added the words "or in a place which is legitimately destined for the confessions of women."

(1) *The Confessional Seat Reserved for Women Religious*

Immediately there arose among the authors the question whether these added words pointed to confessional seats which were located outside a church or oratory and which were reserved exclusively for the confessions of women religious. In other words, did the word *mulierum* as contained in the aforesaid response point exclusively to a place which was destined for the confessions of laywomen who were not women religious? Or did the word point inclusively to a place destined for the confessions both of laywomen of the world and of women religious? The opinion of the authors was divided.

Some authors[22] maintained that the phrase in question did not point to confessional seats which were reserved exclusively for the confessions of women religious. Ferreres (1861-1936) stated even more specifically that in a common confessional, one side of which was destined for use by religious, and the other side of which was destined for use by laywomen of the world, religious could go to confession to an occasional confessor in only that part of the confessional that was reserved for use by laywomen of the world.[23]

These authors argued as follows:

(1) The word *mulieres* in canon 522 certainly refers expressly to laywomen of the world. Therefore in the response of the Pontifical Commission which attempted to clarify the meaning of this canon it should be accepted in this same sense.[24]

---

22. Chelodi, *De Personis*, n. 258; Mahoney, "Confessions of Religious Women in Exceptional Cases," *ER*, LXXIV (1926), 43; Maroto, "Annotationes ad III Responsum," *Commentarium*, II (1921), 36-37; Goyeneche, "De vi can. 522," *Commentarium*, II (1921), 24; Ferreres, *Institutiones Canonicae iuxta novissimum codicem Pii X a Benedicto XV promulgatum iuxtaque praescripta Hispanae disciplinae et Americae Latinae* (2 vols., ed. altera, Barcinone, 1920), I, n. 832 (hereafter cited *Institutiones*); Fanfani, *De Iure Religiosorum*, n. 137.

23. *Institutiones*, I, n. 832.

24. Fanfani, *De Iure Religiosorum*, n. 137; cf. also Maroto, "Annotationes ad III Responsum," *Commentarium*, II (1921), 36-37.

(2) The confessor spoken of in canon 522 has no special jurisdiction for the hearing of the confessions of women religious in accordance with the requirement stated in canon 876, § 1. The quality of the place in which confessions are heard should correspond to the quality of the confessor. Therefore, since the confessor in question is approved simply with reference to the confessions of laywomen of the world, it follows that the designated place for the hearing of confessions should be of a corresponding character.[25]

(3) Women religious who make their confession in the manner which canon 522 makes allowable for them do so after the manner of laywomen of the world. Consequently the place for the hearing of their confessions should also conform to that in which laywomen of the world make their confessions.[26]

(4) If the phrase in question points inclusively to the confessional seat destined for religious, then it was futile and useless for the Code and the response of the Pontifical Commission to make mention of churches, of public or of semi-public oratories, and of other places legitimately destined for the confessions of women. It would have been sufficient to state that such confessions are validly and lawfully made in any place legitimately destined for the confessions of laywomen of the world or of women religious.[27]

It must be conceded that this opinion enjoyed at least extrinsic probability.

Other authors, in holding the contrary position,[28] answered the arguments of their adversaries thus:

(1) It does not follow from the fact that the word *mulieres* in canon 522 refers expressly to laywomen of the world that this word in

25. Maroto, "Annotationes ad III Responsum," *Commentarium,* II (1921), 37.

26. Maroto, *loc. cit.*

27. Fanfani, *De Iure Religiosorum,* n. 137.

28. Cappello, *De Poenitentia,* II, n. 448; Coronata, *Institutiones,* I, 682, note 2; Anonymous, "Pontificiae Commissionis Codici Interpretando Praepositae Responsiones Authenticae," *Jus Pontificium,* III (1923), 119; Vermeersch, "Moralis et Pastoralis Consideratio de Religiosarum Confessione Facta Confessario ex can. 522," *Periodica,* XI (1922), (1)-(8); Prümmer, *Manuale Iuris Canonici in Usum Scholarum* (4. et 5. ed., Friburgi Brisgoviae: B. Herder and Company, 1927), Q. 190 (hereafter cited *Manuale*).

the response of the Pontifical Commission should be accepted in this same sense. In canon 522 this word is used in a generic sense, and the reply of the Pontifical Commission was simply accommodated to the word as it is employed in canon 909, § 1, *oratorio semi-publico mulieribus destinato.* Certainly in this canon the word *mulieribus* has an extensive sense. Furthermore, that which canon 522 grants to a confessor who is approved simply for hearing the confessions of laywomen of the world is to be assumed as granted with even greater reason to a confessor who is approved for hearing the confessions of any women religious. Therefore, if the word *mulieres* has the same extension in both cases, namely in the canon and in the response, that which is affirmed about the place in which are heard the confessions of laywomen of the world holds all the more so in regard to the place in which are heard the confessions of women religious.[29]

(2) Canon 522 is not an exception to canon 876, § 1, but a prescription of law recognized by that very canon. Though canon 876, § 1, states that in the circumstances of canon 522 the confessor of women religious does not need the special approbation of the local ordinary for the hearing of the confession in question, nevertheless it by no means excludes a confessor who possesses such special faculties from acting in virtue of canon 522.[30]

(3) The major premise of the third argument is inexact, for while it is true that religious who avail themselves of the grant of canon 522, on the one hand, and laywomen of the world, on the other hand, are similar in that they can choose their confessor, nevertheless religious are restricted by several conditions, such as motive and approach.[31]

(4) The fourth argument proves too much. If that argumentation were correct, then it would be just as logical to say that, since the response of the Pontifical Commission mentions places legitimately destined for the hearing of confessions, it was futile and useless for the Code and the response to make mention of churches, and of public and semi-public oratories, for the latter are also included in the more in-

---

29. Cf. Cappello, *De Poenitentia,* II, n. 448.

30. McCormick, *Confessors of Religious,* The Catholic University of America Canon Law Studies, n. 33 (Washington, D. C.: The Catholic University of America, 1926), p. 204.

31. McCormick, *Confessors of Religious,* pp. 204-205.

clusive phrase, "places legitimately destined for the hearing of confessions."[32]

Then these authors added further arguments of their own. (1) According to Creusen,[33] there is no such thing as a confessional seat approved exclusively for laywomen of the world. If the confessional seat meets the requirements as enacted in the Code for the confessions of women, then religious may also go to confession there, for they certainly are women. As Creusen says:

> . . . The confessionals in convents satisfy all the conditions required that a woman of the world should be able to confess there: without that a nun could not confess there. For, after all, a nun is a woman. If any difference had to be made, more guarantees would have to be demanded for nuns' confessionals than for those of secular women.[34]

According to a reply of the Sacred Congregation of the Holy Office under date of November 25, 1874,[35] it is certain that the confessionals erected for cloistered nuns are to be considered as true confessionals which can serve for the confessions made by women who rightfully live in the convent and by laywomen of the world who are legitimately within the cloister.

(2) Since nuns are not permitted to leave the enclosure, they could never avail themselves of the privilege conferred by canon 522 if they were not allowed to use the confessional seat in the chapel for their own convent. And yet it is evident that canon 522, by the use of the generic phrase *aliqua religiosa,* and the response of the Pontifical Commission, which used the word *religiosae,* conferred the privilege on all women religious without distinction. Moreover, by its omission of the words *extra domum propriam,* as contained in the decree *Cum de sacramentalibus,* canon 522 intended precisely to confer this favor even upon those who are unable to leave the convent. Therefore the contrary opinion is opposed to the intention of the legislator and could at the same time occasion a grave detriment to nuns.[36]

---

32. McCormick, *op. cit.,* p. 205.
33. "Confessions of Religious Women," *ER,* LXXIV (1926), 507.
34. "Confessions of Religious Women," *ER,* LXXIV (1926), 507-508.
35. S. C. S. Off., 25 nov. 1874—*Fontes,* n. 1033.
36. Cappello, *De Poenitentia,* II, n. 448.

This second opinion, like the first, enjoyed extrinsic probability, and because of its stronger arguments also intrinsic probability. In practice, because of the doubt of law created by these two opposite opinions, such confessions could be heard in any place legitimately destined for women religious, for canon 209 states that the Church supplies jurisdiction in cases of positive and probable doubt.

The whole controversy was finally settled definitively through a response of the Pontifical Commission given under date of December 28, 1927.[37] In the second part of this response it was declared that the word *adeat* is not so to be understood that the confessor cannot be called by the religious herself to a place which is legitimately destined for the confessions of women or of women religious. Today, therefore, there can no longer be any doubt that women religious who make their confession in the manner made allowable for them by canon 522 may do so in any place which is legitimately destined for the confessions of women, even in those places which are reserved exclusively for use by women religious.

(2) *The Confessional Seat in a Church or Oratory*

The words, *in loco ad audiendas confessiones mulierum legitime destinato,* of the response of 1920 also caused doubt in another respect. They are capable of being understood in a twofold sense: (1) They may indicate that the confession is to be heard only in a confessional seat, whether it is located in a church or a public or a semi-public oratory, or in any other place legitimately destined for the hearing of women's confessions. In this sense the interpretation of the response of the Pontifical Commission is declarative insofar as it indicates that religious may use this privilege lawfully and validly in a church or in an oratory only in a confessional seat which is legitimately destined for women's confessions, but it is also extensive insofar as it indicates that they may also avail themselves of this privilege in any place where a confessional seat is legitimately placed for women's confessions. (2) These words may also be interpreted to mean that the confession

---

37. *AAS,* XX (1927), 61; cf. also Bouscaren, *The Canon Law Digest,* I, 296.

may be made validly in any church or public or semi-public oratory apart from its being made necessarily in the confessional seat, and that the confession may be made even in any other place legitimately destined for women's confessions.[38] In this sense the response is purely extensive, and not also declaratory.[39]

The important difference between these two interpretations is readily apparent. According to the first, granted that the element of place is required for the validity of the confession,[40] a confession which is made in a church, or in a public or semi-public oratory, but outside the confessional seat is always invalid. On the other hand, according to the second interpretation, as long as the confession is made in a church, or in a public or semi-public oratory, it is valid, even though it is made unlawfully outside the confessional seat.

Though this question as such is not treated by many authors, their opinion may be deduced from their manner of expression. From this it is easily seen that they are divided, some accepting the first interpretation, and others the second. Sobradillo, arguing for the second interpretation, says that canon 522 is to be interpreted broadly since it confers a privilege. The same holds true for the response of November 24, 1920, given by the Pontifical Commission. On the other hand, the response of December 28, 1927, is to be interpreted strictly since it restricts the favor granted by canon 522, inasmuch as it states that the element of place is required not only for the lawful but even for the valid hearing of the confessions of religious.[41]

Since canon 522 does not specify the details about the element of place, the most that can be said about the confessions of religious made outside the confessional seat in a church, or in a public or semi-public oratory, is that they are unlawful because they violate the general principles concerning the place for the hearing of women's confessions.

---

38. Maroto, "Annotationes ad III Responsum," *Commentarium,* II (1921), 37.

39. Sobradillo, *Tractatus de Religiosarum Confessariis ad Normam Codicis Iuris Canonici Concinnatus* (Taurini, Berrutti, 1932), pp. 207-208 (hereafter cited *De Confessariis*).

40. After the response of the Pontifical Commission on December 28, 1927, there can no longer be any doubt about this.

41. *AAS,* XX (1927), 61; cf. also Bouscaren, *The Canon Law Digest,* I, 296.

Thus, if for some reason a confessional seat had not been erected in a church or in a public or semi-public oratory, as may happen in the case of the oratories of cardinals and bishops, women religious who go to confession therein in accordance with the grant of canon 522 confess validly. However, the confessions thus made are made unlawfully, unless there is a true necessity for hearing them outside a confessional seat.[42] In practice it is certain that, in the light of the statement of canon 209 that the Church supplies jurisdiction in cases of positive and probable doubt, the absolution given in such confessions must be recognized as certainly valid.

The following places outside a church or oratory may be considered as legitimately destined for the confessions of women: (1) confessional seats in hospitals, when erected in some suitable place legitimately destined outside the church or oratory for the convenience of sick women; (2) the same kind of confessional seats located in schools and colleges for the hearing of girls' confessions; (3) in retreat houses, the places appointed legitimately for the confessions of women retreatants; (4) confessional seats in the sacristy or in other places adjacent to the church or oratory when legitimately destined for the confessions of deaf women. Even if the religious is not deaf, she may go to confession in the last mentioned place.[43] In any of the aforementioned places a woman religious, when she avails herself of the grant of canon 522, may confess lawfully.

(3) *The Element of Place Required for Validity*

The response which the Pontifical Commission issued on November 24, 1920, as already stated, did not settle the question whether the place for the hearing of confessions made by religious when utilizing the grant of canon 522 is a necessary element for validity, so that their confessions when heard outside a church, outside a public or semi-public oratory, or outside any other place legitimately destined for the

---

42. Sobradillo, *De Confessariis*, pp. 208-209.

43. Maroto, "Annotationes ad III Responsum," *Commentarium*, II (1921), 38.

confessions of women, would be invalid. Some authors[44] argued that such confessions were valid, while others[45] denied this.

Those who maintained that such confessions were valid used the following arguments:

(1) The circumstance of place is not required for the validity of the confessions of women, and therefore it is not required for the validity of the confessions of religious who utilize the grant of canon 522, for in such cases religious are accommodated in the law after the fashion of laywomen of the world.[46]

(2) The declaration of 1920 states that in the places there mentioned the confessions of religious are lawful and valid. If they are made outside the aforementioned places, it follows that they are unlawful, but it does not follow that they are also invalid.

(3) A similar doubt had existed concerning article 14 of the decree *Cum de sacramentalibus,* and the Sacred Congregation for Religious declared privately to the ordinary of Linz on July 3, 1916, that the word *liceat* of the aforesaid article did not affect the validity of the confessions, nor did it prohibit the hearing of the confession in some other fitting place.[47] The interpretation of canon 522, which canon does not restrict but rather extends the grant made in the former discipline, should follow the favorable interpretation of the earlier law.[48]

---

44. Goyeneche, "De vi can. 522," *Commentarium,* II (1921), 21; Coronata, *Institutiones,* I, 682, note 2; Prümmer, *Manuale,* Q. 190; Vermeersch, "De Confessionum regimine apud religiosos et religiosas," *Periodica,* IX (1921), (15); Sipos, *Enchiridion Iuris Canonici* (3. ed., Pécs: Ex Typographia "Haladás R. T.," 1936), p. 337.

45. Cocchi, *Commentarium in Codicem Iuris Canonici ad Usum Scholarum* (8 vols. in 5, Vol. IV, 3. ed., Taurinorum Augustae: Marietti, 1932), IV, n. 42; Fanfani, *De Iure Religiosorum,* n. 137; Anonymous, "Pontificiae Commissionis Codici Interpretando Praepositae Responsiones Authenticae," *Jus Pontificium,* III (1923), 118; De Meester, *Iuris Canonici et Iuris Canonico-Civilis Compendium* (ed. nova, 3 vols. in 4, Vol. II, Brugis: Desclée de Brouwer et Soc., 1923), II, 417; Vermeersch-Creusen *Epitome,* I, n. 498; Blat, *Commentarium,* Lib. II, Partes II-III, n. 585.

46. Goyeneche, "De vi can. 522," *Commentarium,* II (1921), 21-22.

47. Cf. Leitner, *Handbuch des katholischen Kirchenrechts auf Grund des neuen Kodex* (2 vols., Regensburg: Friederich Pustet, 1919-1927), p. 357.

48. Cf. canon 6, 2°, 3°.

Vermeersch considered this opinion solidly probable,[49] and according to Schaefer (+1948) it was defended in a thesis for the degree of master of arts at the University of Louvain in 1922.[50]

Those who argued that such confessions were invalid offered several arguments: (1) Their principal contention was based on the word *dummodo* contained in the response of November 24, 1920. In pointing to canon 39 they argued that the insertion of the *dummodo* clause, which was omitted in canon 522, implied a *conditio sine qua non* and was equivalent to an explicit declaration that this clause contained mention of a condition essential for validity relative to the specific law interpreted by the Pontifical Commission.[51] (2) The order of words indicates this inasmuch as the response does not say "valid and lawful" but "lawful and valid." (3) The Pontifical Commission expressed its mind privately in favor of this position.[52] The President of the Commission gave a reply, not officially published, to the ordinary of Luxemburg on January 16, 1921, in which it was indicated clearly that the element of place is necessary for validity.

In practice, any religious confessed validly if she approached a confessor who was approved for the hearing of women's confessions and she furthermore confessed lawfully if the confession was made in a church, in a public or a semi-public oratory, or in any other place legitimately destined for women's confessions. This practical conclusion was warranted because the Church supplies jurisdiction in cases of positive and probable doubt.[53]

The controversy continued until a declaration of the Pontifical Commission on December 28, 1927, settled the matter. The Commission was asked "whether the confession of women religious if made outside the places mentioned in canon 522 and in the reply of November

---

49. "De Confessionum regimine apud religiosos et religiosas," *Periodica,* IX (1921), (15).

50. *De Religiosis,* n. 176.

51. Anonymous, "Pontificiae Commissionis Codici Interpretando Praepositae Responsiones Authenticae," *Jus Pontificium,* III (1923), 119.

52. Cf. Bouscaren, *The Canon Law Digest,* I, 295.

53. Cf. canon 209.

24, 1920, is only unlawful or also invalid." It replied, "In the negative to the first part, in the affirmative to the second."[54]

In commenting on this decision shortly after its publication, Creusen regarded it as severe, since it made the validity of jurisdiction for a sacramental act depend upon the legitimate designation of the place in which that act is performed.[55] Goyeneche called the idea something new in law.[56] Sobradillo deemed it strange that the decision was rendered contrary to the very common opinion, but felt that actually it was the desirable decision.[57] For since almost all of the authors had maintained that the element of place was not related to the validity of a confession made under the allowable procedure indicated in canon 522, they were also of the opinion that a place chosen in a particular case by a confessor in accordance with the prescriptions of canon 910, § 1, was a legitimately destined place, and that accordingly women religious could validly and lawfully go to confession therein. Such an opinion gave grounds for believing that any reason at all was to be considered sufficient for hearing the confessions of women religious when utilizing the grant of canon 522 outside the legitimately destined place, e. g., in parlors. The response of the Pontifical Commission also served to prevent abuses of the privilege conferred in canon 522.[58]

Perhaps the Pontifical Commission would not have rendered this decision, thus Sobradillo opined, if authors had not disputed the question whether the element of place relates only to the factor of lawfulness or also to the factor of validity, and also examined the question, as did Maroto (1875-1937),[59] whether a place chosen by the confessor in a particular case in accordance with the prescriptions of canon 910, § 1, is to be considered as a legitimately destined place.[60]

---

54. *AAS,* XX (1927), 61; cf. also Bouscaren, *The Canon Law Digest,* I, 296. Translation by the writer.

55. "Confesseur Occasionnel des Religieuses," *Nouvelle Revue Théologique* (Tournai, 1869-), LXII (1935), 513.

56. "De Confessione Religiosarum," *Apollinaris,* VIII (1935), 557.

57. *De Confessariis,* p. 214.

58. Sobradillo, *op. cit.,* pp. 214-215.

59. "Annotationes ad III Responsum," *Commentarium,* II (1921), 38.

60. Sobradillo, *De Confessariis,* p. 215.

In regard to this latter question, even after the response of 1927, Maroto continued to hold the opinion he had expressed just after the response of 1920 was published. At that time he said:

> Si ad normam can. 910 in casu verae necessitatis et adhibitis cautelis ab Ordinario loci praescriptis confessarius pro mulieribus approbatus recipiat alicuius religiosae confessionem extra sedem confessionalem in loco ubi reciperet in pari casu mulierum saecularium confessiones, legitime destinatus pariter censendus est ille locus, quoniam ab ipso confessario et a religiosa poenitente eligitur ad normam legis, id est canonis 910 et iuxta cautelas ab Ordinario statutas; cum enim tunc religiosa instituat confessionem more saecularium mulierum, cur non poterit frui favore per can. 910 mulieribus saecularibus concesso?[61]

Sobradillo[62] and Creusen[63] conceded to the opinion of Maroto great probability before the response of 1927. However, after this same response, Sobradillo said that the contrary opinion was to be preferred to Maroto's, while Creusen believed Maroto's opinion to be excluded absolutely.

Sobradillo argued that the Pontifical Commission meant that a place legitimately destined for the hearing of confessions was to be understood as the confessional, at least whenever this was found outside a church or a public or semi-public oratory. And a place chosen in a particular case according to the prescriptions of canon 910, § 1, does not come under the name of a confessional, for the canon distinguishes between these two by using the words *extra sedem confessionalem*.[64] Thus, according to Creusen, a religious who is not gravely ill and therefore may not avail herself of the use of canon 523, and who is unable to go to confession to a place destined for the hearing of women's confessions, could make her confession only to a confessor who has special jurisdiction. The reason is that the place *extra sedem*

61. Maroto, "Annotationes ad III Responsum," *Commentarium*, II (1921), 38; cf. also Maroto, "Pontificia Commissio ad Codicis Canones Authentice Interpretandos," — *ibid.*, IX (1928), 96.

62. *De Confessariis*, p. 211.

63. "Les Dernières Réponses de la Commission d'Interprétation du Code," *Nouvelle Revue Théologique*, LV (1928), 281.

64. Sobradillo, *De Confessariis*, p. 211.

confessionalem in which she would have to confess because of illness is not a legitimately destined place.[65] Maroto, on the other hand, said that such a place is legitimately destined, for wherever an approved priest lawfully hears the confession of a laywoman of the world the place is in consequence of the ruling contained in canon 910, § 1, lawfully destined also for a woman religious who makes her confession under the same circumstances.[66]

The opponents of Maroto's opinion further argued that it would lead to the very abuses which the Pontifical Commission wished to prevent by means of its declaration of 1927 which postulated the element of place for the validity of a confession made within what according to canon 522 was allowable.[67]

The opinion and the very terminology of the opinion of Maroto was confirmed when the problem was solved definitively in a response of the Pontifical Commission under date of February 12, 1935. The Pontifical Commission was asked:

> Whether the words, *loco legitime destinato,* which were the subject of the interpretation of canon 522 on November 24, 1920, are to be understood only of a place habitually designated, or also of a place designated on and for a single occasion, or chosen in accordance with canon 910, § 1.

It replied, "In the negative to the first part; in the affirmative to the second."[68]

Relative to the element of place, the following practical conclusions may be drawn with regard to the validity of confessions when made in accordance with the grant of canon 522 by religious to a confessor approved for hearing the confessions of women:

(1) Wherever the confession of a laywoman of the world may be heard lawfully, a woman religious may be heard validly. But the complete reversal of this statement is not true. Therefore it is incorrect to

65. "Les Dernières Réponses de la Commission d'Interprétation du Code," *Nouvelle Revue Théologique,* LV (1928), 280.

66. "Annotationes ad III Responsum," *Commentarium,* II (1921), 38.

67. Sobradillo, *De Confessariis,* p. 211.

68. *AAS,* XXVII (1935), 92; cf. also Bouscaren, *The Canon Law Digest,* II, 161. Translation by the writer.

say that, if a laywoman of the world confesses unlawfully inasmuch as the confession occurs in an unlawful place, then a woman religious confesses invalidly in that place.

(2) The confession is valid if it is made anywhere in a church, or in a public or a semi-public oratory, or if it is made in any place legitimately destined for the confessions of women, or also in any other place legitimately chosen by the confessor or penitent for that particular occasion.

(3) If the confessor has the special faculties necessary for hearing the confessions of women religious, he always hears them validly, regardless of place. For lawfulness, however, the general rules for the confessions of women must be followed.[69]

(4) *The Sacristy*

When canon 522 permits the confession of a woman religious to an occasional confessor to be heard in any church or public or semi-public oratory, is the sacristy to be considered a part of the church or oratory so that such a confession may be made validly and lawfully therein? The better opinion seems to be that which denies that the sacristy is a part of the church, whether it is contiguous to or separated from the church. For, to consider the sacristy as part of the church or the oratory in this particular case implies more than simply a broad interpretation of these terms; it entails in reality an extensive interpretation, which according to canon 17, § 1, is reserved exclusively to the legislator or his delegate.[70]

However, the opinion of those who affirm that the confessions of women religious may be made in the sacristy is not without probability. They argue that in favorable matters the sacristy is to be considered as part of the church, even though they admit that in the strict rigor of the canons wherein the sacristy is mentioned incidentally it seems to be

---

69. Woywod, "Sacramental Confession of Sisters," *The Homiletic and Pastoral Review* (New York, 1900-), XXXVI (1936), 871 (hereafter cited *HPR*).

70. Sobradillo, *De Confessariis,* p. 206.

regarded as a place distinct from the church or the oratory.[71] In practice this more lenient opinion may be followed, provided that the general principles regarding the confessions of women are observed.

There is no doubt that a woman religious who utilizes the grant of canon 522 may go to confession lawfully in a sacristy in which there is a confessional seat legitimately destined for the confessions of women, e. g., the deaf. It is also certain that if the confessor hears the confession of a woman religious in the sacristy as a place lawfully chosen for a specific occasion in accordance with the ruling of canon 910, § 1, the confession is valid and lawful.

If the door of the sacristy has a hole cut through it and is equipped with a screen so as to serve as a confessional in such a way that the woman religious is in the oratory and the confessor is in the sacristy, the confession made in such a place is to be considered lawful. For the actual confession is made in the oratory, even though the absolution is given in the sacristy, and according to the strict letter of the law canon 522 refers to the place where the religious makes her confession.[72]

A revolving servidor[73] which in an adjoining sacristy is built into the wall that divides the sacristy from the church or the oratory, does not strictly seem to be an unlawful place for the hearing of the confession of a woman religious, even though it does not serve as an apt place for confessions because of the absence of a screen as also because of its possible revolving motion. In line with the argument — which possesses sufficient probability — that in favorable matters the sacristy may be considered as part of the church, it may be said that a confession made through such a servidor by a woman religious on the inside (i. e., in

71. Regatillo, *Ius Sacramentarium,* I, n. 462; Cappello, *De Poenitentia,* II, n. 444; Raus, *Institutiones Canonicae iuxta Novum Codicem Iuris pro Scholis vel ad Usum Privatum synthetice Redactae* (2. ed., Lugduni-Parisiis: Typis Emmanuelis Vitte, 1931), n. 181.

72. Regatillo, *Ius Sacramentarium,* I, n. 462.

73. This is a hollow, cylindrical, revolvable structure (*rota*) which, fitted out with one or more platform levels, is installed in the wall at the gate of the monastery, in the sacristy wall, or wherever it is needed. Through it necessary articles may be passed. It may even have a little opening through which one may see what is being put into it. Cf. S. C. de Religiosis, *Instructio de Clausura Monialium Votorum Solemnium,* 6 febr. 1924 — *AAS,* XVI (1924), 97; cf. also Bouscaren, *The Canon Law Digest,* I, 315.

the convent) to a confessor seated on the other side (i. e., in the sacristy) could also be considered as being made in the sacristy. According to some documents regarding confession, reference is made directly to the place where the confession is made or where it is heard. For example, the reply of the Pontifical Commission on November 24, 1920, stated that "Canon 522 is so to be understood that the confessions . . . are lawful and valid provided they are *made* in a church, or in an oratory, even a semi-public one, or in a place legitimately destined for the *hearing* of confessions."[74] Therefore, inasmuch as the confession is heard in the sacristy, even though it is actually made outside the sacristy, it may be considered lawful.

B. THE CONFESSION OF NUNS

Under ordinary circumstances the confessor is bound to observe the laws of the cloister. Therefore the confessional seat must be so located as to allow the penitents to remain within the enclosure and the confessor outside it. A permanent grating placed in an opening in the wall of the chapel, of the sacristy, or of the choir, is canonically acceptable if the general principles regarding the confessions of women are also observed.[75] Only the ordinary confessor, the extraordinary confessor, an appointed confessor, or one who is called by a seriously ill nun who uses the privilege which canon 523 concedes to her, are allowed to enter the cloister to hear the confession of a sick nun.[76] Since the occasional confessor is not mentioned in the *Instructio* as enjoying this right, he may not enter the cloister.[77] Whenever a nun's confession is heard in her cell, then as a precaution it is prescribed that two nuns accompany the confessor to the cell of the sick nun and wait there before the open door of the cell while the priest

74. Regatillo, *loc. cit.* Translation and italics by the writer.

75. S. C. de Religiosis, *Instr. de Clausura,* 6 febr. 1924 — *AAS,* XVI (1924), 97; cf. also Bouscaren, *The Canon Law Digest,* I, 315.

76. S. C. de Religiosis, *Instr. de Clausura,* 6 febr. 1924 — *AAS,* XVI, (1924), 99; cf. also Bouscaren, *The Canon Law Digest,* I, 318.

77. Berutti, *Institutiones Iuris Canonici* (6 vols., Vol. III, Taurini-Romae: Marietti, 1936-), III, 46 (hereafter cited *Institutiones*).

hears the confession, and accompany him again when he returns to the monastery gate.[78]

ARTICLE 2. *The Confession of Men Religious*

The privilege which canon 519 grants to men religious, namely to approach any approved confessor whenever the confession is made for the peace of their conscience, corresponds to that which canon 522 grants to women religious. However, in canon 519 the restrictive phrase "in any church or oratory, even a semi-public one" is not found, for according to canon 910, § 2, the confessions of men may be heard lawfully even in private homes, while according to canon 909, § 1, the confessional seat for the confessions of women is to be placed generally in a church or in a public or semi-public oratory.

There are no special prescriptions of law, therefore, regarding the place in which the confessions of men religious are to be heard. In the matter of the hearing of their confessions the same principles apply to them that apply to laymen.

78. S. C. de Religiosis, *Instr. de Clausura*, 6 febr. 1924—*AAS*, XVI (1924), 99; cf. also Bouscaren, *The Canon Law Digest*, I, 318.

CHAPTER VI

RIGHTS AND DUTIES OF THE LOCAL ORDINARY

ARTICLE 1. *His Authority to Designate Places for the Hearing of Confessions*

Neither the Code nor any of the responses of the Pontifical Commission explicitly reserve to the local ordinary the right of designating the place for the hearing of confessions. However, according to the prescription of canon 910, § 1, which recognizes explicitly the power of the ordinary to prescribe the precautions that are to be taken when the confessions of women are heard outside the confessional seat, and also according to canon 336, § 2, which asserts the bishop's duty to prevent abuses in the administration of the sacraments, the local ordinary at least implicitly is accorded the right to designate the places for the hearing of the confessions of women outside churches and oratories.[1]

Most of the commentators reserve the general right of designation to the bishop or to the local ordinary as the competent authority.[2] Some writers[3] find fault with the opinion of Cappello, who, though agreeing with the general principle that the right of designation belongs generally to the bishop or to the local ordinary as the competent superior, states that in a particular and extraordinary case the place may be designated legitimately here and now by the confessor himself or by the superioress or by some other person.[4] This difference of opinion is easily reconciled if it is understood that the confessor or the superioress or the penitent may choose the place of confession according

1. Fallon, "Canon 522 and Confession of a Nun in a Sacristy," *The Irish Ecclesiastical Record* (Dublin, 1864-), 5. series, XLIX (1937), 314 (hereafter cited *IER*).

2. It also seems correct to say that the superior of a clerical exempt institute may designate legitimately the place which is intended for the hearing of the confessions, not of the faithful in general, but of religious.

3. E. g., Fallon, "Canon 522 and Confession of a Nun in a Sacristy," *IER*, 5. series, XLIX (1937), 314.

4. *De Poenitentia,* II, n. 450.

to canon 910, § 1, but that the legitimate designation comes from the law itself by the very fact that its requirements are fulfilled. This opinion seems warranted by the response of the Pontifical Commission on February 12, 1935, which stated that a legitimately destined place is not only one which is habitually destined but also one which is designated on and for a specific occasion, or is chosen according to the prescriptions of canon 910, § 1. In all cases it is the designation of the place which makes it to be a lawful place for the hearing of confessions.[5]

Though the designation of the place for the hearing of confessions ordinarily belongs to the local ordinary, the actual act of designation need not be made through his immediate and direct intervention in each individual case. It is sufficient if he prescribes the general conditions to be observed and any mandatory special safeguards which in his prudent judgment he deems necessary or advisable.[6]

Once these conditions are actually observed, the place *ipso facto* becomes designated lawfully. It matters not whether the designation is made habitually, v. g., with reference to a church, or on some specific occasion or in some particular cases, v. g., with reference to a retreat. The ordinary may inspect the place which is used for the hearing of confessions, and his approval, whether explicit or implicit, even tacit, constitutes the place as one legitimately designated. He may also entrust the act of designation to a delegate, for example to the pastor or the rector, as the proper and immediate superior of the place. The designation may also be made lawfully by the confessor himself in those exceptional cases envisioned in canon 910, § 1.

As already explained, if a religious in utilizing the grant of canon 522 makes her confession outside the confessional seat because of infirmity or necessity, either she or the confessor may choose the place, and this is to be considered a lawful designation if it is made in accord with the ruling of canon 910, § 1. Since canon 909, § 1, states that the confessional seat for women is generally to be located in a church, or in

5. Goyeneche, "De Confessione Religiosarum," *Apollinaris,* VIII (1935), 557.

6. Maroto, "Annotationes ad III Responsum," *Commentarium, II* (1921), 38.

a public oratory, or even in a semi-public oratory to which they have the right of free access, it clearly, by reason of the term "generally," allows the ordinary to designate for a just and reasonable cause some other place, such as a private oratory.[7] This is also evident from the use of the word *proprius* in canon 908, a term which does not have the sense of exclusiveness. Therefore, following the prescriptions of the general law, the local ordinary may designate for a just reason any place as a place for the hearing of confessions.

ARTICLE 2. *His Power to Enact Penal Sanctions*

In addition to his power to designate places for the hearing of confessions, the local ordinary also has the right to enact penal sanctions for violations. Those penalties, however, should not be over-severe.[8]

The local ordinary may even impose conditions which affect the validity of the confession heard, since it is entirely within his right to delegate jurisdiction for the hearing of confessions and to circumscribe that jurisdiction within certain limits, whether in regard to time, persons, or territory. However, he may not restrict any of the liberties granted by the Code. Any particular restriction which runs counter to a prescription of the Code is unlawful. Thus it is certain that the local ordinary may not forbid the confessions of women religious to be heard in a confessional seat where the confessions of laywomen of the world are heard. For it is by a direct authorization of the Church's universal law that women religious are permitted to confess in those places which are legitimately destined for the confessions of laywomen of the world.

---

7. Berutti, *Institutiones*, III, n. 46.

8. Cf. the directive issued by the Sacred Congregation of Bishops and Regulars in 1719 to the Bishop of Cagli to abolish the suspension *a divinis* incurred *ipso facto* by a confessor who heard confessions outside the church, except in a case of infirmity, and by those who, while hearing the confessions of women in church, nevertheless heard them outside the confessional, and instead merely to suspend such a priest from the hearing of confessions. — Bizzarri, *Collectanea*, p. 341.

In delegating jurisdiction for the hearing of the confessions of laywomen of the world, the local ordinary likewise may not forbid the confessor to hear the confession of a woman religious who approaches him in accordance with the privilege which canon 522 grants her. Once this jurisdiction is granted, canon 522 allows a woman religious to approach such a confessor, and therefore the local ordinary cannot declare invalid the use of this jurisdiction.[9] Thus, the contrary opinion of Mahoney notwithstanding,[10] an ordinary cannot declare that he grants jurisdiction for the hearing of women's confessions only in churches and not in semi-public oratories. For once all the conditions prescribed by the Code are present, the faithful are using a right which is granted to them by the Holy See, and which accordingly remains immune from restrictions on the part of the local ordinary.[11]

The local ordinary could, however, require for validity that the confessions of women be heard in a church or in a public or semi-public oratory, even though the common law of the Code requires this only for lawfulness. Such action is not contrary to the Code for it is not the restriction of any right held through the law of the Code; it is rather the intensification of the very law upon which the Code has already conferred its approval. It must be admitted, however, that the Church seems to be averse to having a particular legislator attach an invalidating clause to legislation regarding the hearing of confessions. Thus, for example, when in 1725 the Bishop of the Vicariate of Tunkin ordered under pain of invalidity that a reed-screen with small perforations be used for the hearing of women's confessions, the Holy Office commanded him to amend the decree so that priests would be forbidden simply to hear the confessions of women without such a screen when it could conveniently be had, mention of all penalties being omitted, especially that which affected the validity of the confession.[12]

---

9. Creusen, "Confessions des Religieuses," *Nouvelle Revue Théologique*, LV (1928), 766-767.

10. "Confessions of Religious Women in Exceptional Cases," *ER*, LXXIV (1926), 44.

11. Creusen, "Confessions of Religious Women," *ER*, LXXIV (1926), 508.

12. S. C. S. Off., 28 nov. 1725, ad 8 — *Fontes*, n. 785.

ARTICLE 3. *His Right of Canonical Visitation*

A) PAROCHIAL CHURCHES

According to canon 343, § 1, the bishop must every five years visit his entire diocese either personally or through a delegate.[13] The objects of this visitation include persons, places and things.[14] Numbered among these, therefore, are churches, chapels, confessionals and confessional seats.

As regards the visitation of parochial churches connected in any way with religious,[15] secular churches are completely subject to the local ordinary's visitation, even though the parish is under the charge of religious or is incorporated with a religious house.

As regards the churches of regulars, while they are exempt according to canon 615, nevertheless if these churches are parochial churches they become subject to the jurisdiction and visitation of the local ordinary insofar as they serve the parish.[16] It is the common teaching of canonists that all the churches of regulars which are also parochial churches are subject to the visitation of the local ordinary in all things which concern the care of souls.[17]

---

13. The III Plenary Council of Baltimore (1884) ordered this to be done every three years, a decree which is still in effect. — *Acta et Decreta Concilii Plenarii Baltimorensis Tertii,* A. D. 1884 (Baltimorae: Typis Ioannis Murphy et Sociorum, 1886), n. 14.

14. Canon 344, § 1.

15. "Parishes connected in some way to religious may first of all be classified as religious or secular parishes. The religious parish is one incorporated (united) *pleno iure* with a religious house, i. e., united in regard to matters spiritual and temporal. The secular parish is either incorporated (united) *quoad temporalia tantum* or is in spiritual affairs under at least the temporary charge of religious clergy." — Reilly, *The Visitation of Religious,* The Catholic University of America Canon Law Studies, n. 112 (Washington, D. C.: The Catholic University of America, 1938), p. 130.

16. Reilly, *The Visitation of Religious,* p. 137.

17. Cf. Fanfani, *De Iure Religiosorum,* n. 449; Vromant, "De Regimine Paroeciarum et Quasi-Paroeciarum Religiosis Sodalibus Concreditarum," *Jus Pontificium,* XIII (1933), 280; Benedictus XIV, const. *Firmandis,* 6 nov. 1744, § 7 — *Fontes,* n. 349.

B) HOUSES OF RELIGIOUS PROFESSED WITH SIMPLE VOWS[18]

1) Religious of Diocesan Approval

According to canon 512, § 1, 2°, the local ordinary is obliged to make a visitation every five years,[19] personally or through his delegate, of every religious institute, whether of men or of women, which is of diocesan approval. Since he proceeds with unlimited power of inquiry and inspection,[20] he may investigate all matters which concern the administration of the sacrament of penance. Not the least important among the points of examination is an inspection of the actual place in which confessions are heard, whether it relates to the confessions of the religious themselves or of the faithful.

2) Religious of Pontifical Approval

Though religious congregations of pontifical approval, both clerical and lay, enjoy a considerable measure of independence, nevertheless in many points they are subject to the jurisdiction of the local ordinary. In respect to those things which have some reference to the place for the hearing of confessions the local ordinary has the right and the duty to visit every five years[21] the church, the public oratory, the sacristy, and the confessional seat. This he may do with regard to both clerical and lay congregations, even if the congregation is exempt.[22]

---

18. With regard to the visitation of religious by their own superiors, canon 511 states that the major religious superiors whom the constitutions designate as visitors shall at the times determined by the constitutions visit all the houses which are subject to them. In making the visitation, these major superiors have the duty to examine all the places in which confessions are heard.

19. Decree n. 14 of the III Plenary Council of Baltimore (1884), which requires a triennial visitation of the diocese, does not apply with regard to the visitation of the houses of religious.

20. Fanfani, *De Iure Religiosorum*, n. 70.

21. As in the case of the houses of congregations of diocesan approval, decree n. 14 of the III Plenary Council of Baltimore (1884), which requires a visitation of the diocese every three years, does not apply in this case.

22. Cf. canon 512, § 2, 2°, 3°.

It matters not whether the church be parochial or non-parochial in character. It is subject to the visitation of the local ordinary. The confessional seat of which canon 512, § 2, 2°, speaks is that which is destined for the confessions of the faithful, even though it is located in a church or in a public oratory. Semi-public oratories[23] and confessional seats erected for the benefit, not of the faithful in general, but of religious, are not included in the ambit of the local ordinary's visitation.[24]

C) MONASTERIES AND CONVENTS OF REGULARS

1) Nuns Subject to the Local Ordinary or Immediately Subject to the Holy See

Canon 512, § 1, 1°, imposes upon the local ordinary the duty of making a quinquennial visitation of the monasteries of nuns who are under his own jurisdiction or who are immediately subject to the Holy See. Except for the fact that in visiting the former the local ordinary acts in virtue of his own ordinary jurisdiction, while in visiting the latter he acts by vicarious apostolic authority, there is no juridical distinction between those two cases with regard to the act of visitation. In both cases the powers of the local ordinary as visitator are identical.

In making his visitation the local ordinary is bound to observe the laws of the cloister. Therefore he may enter the cloister only for the purpose of inspection, and he must be accompanied by at least one cleric or male religious of mature age.[25] He has the right and the obligation of inspecting any and all confessional seats wherever they may be located.

---

23. Coronata favors the subjection to the local ordinary of semi-public oratories of non-exempt clerical religious, since otherwise they would seem not to come under the jurisdiction of any visitor. — *Institutiones*, I, 668, note 2.

24. Larraona, "Commentarium Codicis," *Commentarium*, VIII (1927), 447; Goyeneche, "Consultationes," *Commentarium*, III (1922), 335-336.

25. Cf. canon 600, 1°.

2) *Nuns Subject to Regulars*

With regard to the monasteries of nuns who are subject to regulars, canon 512, § 2, 1°, states that every five years the local ordinary must visit them in those matters which have reference to the laws of the cloister. Since it is required by law that the confessional seat be located in such a way that the confessor remains outside the cloister while the nun remains within it, this obviously is a matter which relates to the laws of the cloister. Therefore the local ordinary has the obligation to inspect the confessional seat in order to determine if it conforms to the law.

3) *Male Regulars*

The local ordinary does not possess the right to visit the houses of religious orders of men. Canon 615 states that regulars, both men and women, including novices, except those nuns who are not subject to regular superiors, are exempt, together with their houses and churches, from the jurisdiction of the local ordinary, except in the cases for which the law makes other provision. Furthermore, the bishop may visit exempt religious with regard to only those cases or matters for which the law has expressly warranted his act of visitation.[26] All canonists agree that neither in canon 512, which deals with the visitation of religious, nor elsewhere in the Code, is the local ordinary given the right to visit the houses of religious orders of men.[27]

The only right of visitation which the local ordinary possesses with regard to the houses of male regulars is stated in canon 1261. This canon states that if the local ordinary has enacted laws for his territory through which he seeks to curb abuses in divine worship, superstitious practices, traditions, or anything which has the appearance of shameful gain, then all religious, even though they be exempt, are bound to observe these laws; and for the achievement of this purpose the local ordinary may visit their churches and public oratories.

This visitation, however, may be made only when the local ordinary has positive knowledge that the particular laws which he enacted

---

26. Cf. canon 344, § 2.

27. Cf. Fanfani, *De Iure Religiosorum*, n. 70.

are not being observed in the churches of the regulars or of other religious who by privilege enjoy a like exemption.[28] Therefore, if the local ordinary has passed such laws with regard to the hearing of confessions or the confessional seat, and if he has positive knowledge, not a mere suspicion, that these laws are not being observed in the churches of regulars or of other equally exempt religious, he may lawfully make a visitation of these houses with regard to the observance of his law.

Coronata states that, if the local ordinary gives rules which determine more specifically the general law with regard to the erection and location of confessional seats, then even exempt religious are obliged to observe these norms in hearing the confessions of the laity.[29] It must be added that such an established obligation connotes the right of the ordinary's visitation simply within the provisions of law already explained.

D) HOUSES OF QUASI-RELIGIOUS

The provisions of canon 512 with reference to the visitation by the local ordinary of diocesan congregations, of exempt and non-exempt clerical congregations of pontifical approval, and of lay congregations

---

28. Cardinal Gasparri in his capacity as President of the Pontifical Commission declared in reply to several doubts: 1) that the laws referred to in canon 1261 are not to be identified with diocesan laws which merely reaffirm the general laws of the Church; rather, they point to diocesan laws which have a content entirely distinct from that of the law already enacted in the Code; 2) that the visitation mentioned in canon 1261, § 2, is not the ordinary quinquennial visitation; 3) that the referred-to visitation may be made only when the local ordinary has positive knowledge that particular laws passed by him are not being observed in the churches of the regulars or of other similarly exempt religious. Cf. Bouscaren, *The Canon Law Digest,* II, 374-375.

Though this response was not promulgated in the *Acta Apostolicae Sedis,* there should be no doubt about its being an authentic interpretation. According to canon 17, § 2, an authentic interpretation which declares the meaning of words which in themselves are certain in their meaning needs no promulgation, and it is fully acknowledged that the President of the Pontifical Commission acting alone may give an authentic interpretation to doubts which are of lesser importance or which offer no great difficulty. Cf. "Pontificia Commissio ad Codicis Canones Authentice Interpretandos," *AAS,* XI (1919), 480, nota 1.

29. *De Sacramentis,* I, n. 463.

of pontifical approval, apply equally as well in virtue of canon 674 to societies whose members live the common life apart from the profession of religious vows. Therefore the local ordinary may inspect their churches, public oratories, sacristies, and confessional seats.

CHAPTER VII

MISCELLANEOUS QUESTIONS

ARTICLE 1. *Solicitation*

It is not within the purpose of this work to treat in a detailed manner the question of solicitation. Rather, it is intended merely to consider the element of place as one of the conditions postulated before this delict is committed and the canonical penalties attached to it are incurred.[1] In setting down the obligation of the penitent to denounce a confessor who is guilty of solicitation, canon 904 explicitly incorporates as law the constitution *Sacramentum Poenitentiae,* issued by Benedict XIV on June 1, 1741. With reference to the place where the solicitation occurs, this Constitution states that the delict is committed

> . . . even outside the occasion of confession in a confessional, or in any other place destined or chosen for the hearing of confessions, if the hearing of confession is simulated there. . . .[2]

Authors are agreed that two conditions must be verified concurrently, namely the circumstance of place and the simulation of confession. It is certain, therefore, that if the simulation of confession along with the solicitation takes place in a confessional, or in any other place habitually destined for the hearing of confessions, as these terms have already been explained, the delict is committed and the solicited penitent is obliged to denounce the delinquent confessor. With regard to a confessor who solicits in a place chosen for the specific occasion for simulating the hearing of a single confession, some authors maintain, and rightly so, that the delict is not committed in such a case.[3] For the papal Constitution speaks of the simulation of confession and of the act of solicitation when they occur in a place chosen *for the hearing*

1. Cf. canon 2368.
2. Benedictus XIV, const. *Sacramentum Poenitentiae,* 1 iun. 1741, § 1 — *Codex Iuris Canonici Pii X Pontificis Maximi iussu digestus Benedicti XV auctoritate promulgatus* (Romae: Typis Polyglottis Vaticanis, 1917), Documentum V, § 1. Translation by the writer.
3. Cf. Cerato, *De Delicto Sollicitationis,* n. 47.

of confessions, which phrase cannot be understood of a place chosen for the simulated hearing of a confession. In practice, since there is question of a canonical penalty, the phrase must be interpreted strictly.[4]

ARTICLE 2. *Confessions during Journeys in the Air*

In a *Motu Proprio,* issued by His Holiness Pope Pius XII on January 28, 1948, canon 883 regarding the faculty for the hearing of confessions on the part of priests taking a sea voyage was extended, under the same terms and conditions, to priests making a journey by air.[5] Priests, however, who avail themselves of either of these concessions must observe the general rules regarding the place for the hearing of confessions. Since ordinarily there will be no accommodations aboard a plane for the hearing of confessions, the priest himself will be obliged to choose a suitable place on and for the emerging occasion. In the case of women the specific ruling of canon 910, § 1, must be duly observed.

ARTICLE 3. *The Place for the Hearing of Confessions in the Oriental Church*

Until the new codification of Oriental Canon Law appears, the practice in the Oriental Church concerning the place for the hearing of confessions is to be regulated by the decrees of the Sacred Congregations which apply to Orientals and by the particular laws, both synodal and provincial, which obtain within the various rites. Though the fundamental reasons that underlie the canonical legislation with regard to the place for the hearing of confessions as formulated in the Latin Church apply equally well in the Oriental Church, and therefore even *a priori* one does not expect substantial differences between the practice in the two Churches, nevertheless Orientals are not bound by the law of the Code in this matter. And from the examples given in the historical part of this work with reference to the legislation which emanated from the Roman Pontiffs, the Sacred Roman Congregations, and

4. Cf. canon 19.
5. *AAS,* XL (1948), 17.

the particular Oriental Churches — legislation which substantially remains in effect even today — it is rightly concluded that today there is no substantial difference in the general discipline and practice that obtain in the Oriental and in the Latin Churches with regard to the place for the hearing of confessions.

SUMMARY OF CONCLUSIONS

1. There is proof from the beginning of the ninth century that confessions were regularly heard in churches, except in cases of sickness or necessity, when they could be heard in any open, decent and apt place. In such cases some precautions were always to be taken if the penitent was a woman. These safeguards were to be invoked through having witnesses in attendance, through leaving the door of the room open when confessions were heard in a private home, through having the confessor use his surplice sleeve or a handkerchief to shield his face, or through having the woman veil her face. Though the place was to be open to the view of the bystanders, the latter were never to be within hearing range. After confessionals were introduced by St. Charles Borromeo in 1576, it was not allowed to hear women's confessions outside a church's confessional equipped with a minutely perforated metal grille, except for reasons of illness, deafness, or necessity. The most important precaution to be taken in all cases was the use of the grille, which separated the confessor from the penitent. Ordinaries had the duty of vigilance over the place for the hearing of confessions and the right to enact penalties for the violation of their prescriptions in regard to it.

2. As early as the ninth century the regular place for the confessions of nuns was the confessional seat located in the convent church. Only in illness could they be heard in their cells. Some precautions were always required in these cases, such as the requirement that the confessor have a companion or that he leave the cell door open.

3. From the latter part of the sixteenth century there is evidence to show that confessions could also be heard in public and private oratories, always with the necessary previous permission.

4. Though the proper place for the hearing of confessions is a church, or a public or a semi-public oratory, and though these are in general sacred places, it does not follow that every sacred place is a proper place for the hearing of confessions.

5. Any place legitimately designated, whether habitually or individually for the occasion, is lawfully destined for the hearing of confessions.

6. The term "confessional seat" (*sedes confessionalis*) as used in the Code is a term which points to a place habitually destined for the hearing of confessions.

7. Infirmity or illness on the part of the confessor is a sufficient reason in warrant of his hearing a woman's confession outside the confessional seat.

8. The ultimate judge of true necessity which requires the confession of a woman to be heard outside the confessional seat is the confessor.

9. A relative norm, such as the devotional habits of the penitent, may be used as the basis for determining the necessity of hearing a woman's confession outside the confessional seat.

10. As regards the element of place, the validity of a confession is affected only in the case of a woman religious who confesses to an occasional confessor.

11. Wherever the confession of a laywoman of the world can be heard lawfully, there also the confession of a woman religious who utilizes the grant of canon 522 can under the same circumstances be heard validly. But if a laywoman of the world confesses unlawfully inasmuch as she makes her confession in an unlawful place, it does not follow that a woman religious confesses invalidly in that place.

12. It seems to be the desire of the Church that the penalties which the local ordinary enacts for violations regarding the place for the hearing of confessions should be restrained in their character.

13. Though the local ordinary has the power to attach an invalidating clause to his regulation concerning the element of place when he grants faculties for the hearing of confessions, it appears to be the mind of the Church that he should do so only very rarely.

BIBLIOGRAPHY

Sources

Acta Apostolicae Sedis, Commentarium Officiale, Romae, 1909- .

Acta et Decreta Concilii Plenarii Americae Latinae anno 1899 Romae Celebrati, 2 vols., Romae, 1902.

Acta et Decreta Concilii Plenarii Australasiae Primi, anno 1885, Sydney, 1887.

Acta et Decreta Concilii Plenarii Baltimorensis Tertii, A. D. 1884, Baltimorae: Typis Ioannis Murphy et Sociorum, 1886.

Acta et Decreta Sacrorum Conciliorum Recentiorum, Collectio Lacensis, 7 vols., Friburgi Brisgoviae, 1870-1892.

Acta et Statuta Primae Synodi Dioecesanae Ultrajectensis, Gestel St. Michaelis, 1867.

Acta et Statuta Synodi Richmondiensis Secundae Mense Aug. A. D. 1886 Celebratae, Baltimorae, 1886.

Acta Synodi Roffensis Tertiae Quam die IX Junii 1914 in Ecclesia Cathedrali S. Patricii Roffae [Episcopus] celebravit, Roffae, 1914.

Borromeo, Sanctus Carolus a, *Acta Ecclesiae Mediolanensis,* 2 vols., Lugduni, 1682-1683.

Bouscaren, T. Lincoln, *The Canon Law Digest,* 2 vols., Milwaukee: Bruce, 1934-1943.

Bullarii Romani Continuatio Summorum Pontificum, 14 vols., Prati, 1845-1856.

Codex Iuris Canonici Pii X Pontificis Maximi iussu digestus Benedicti XV auctoritate promulgatus, Romae: Typis Polyglottis Vaticanis, 1917.

Codicis Iuris Canonici Fontes, cura Emi Petri Card. Gasparri editi, 9 vols., Romae (postea Civitate Vaticana): Typis Polyglottis Vaticanis, 1923-1939. (Vols. VII, VIII et IX ed. cura et studio Emi Iustiniani Card. Serédi.)

Codificazione Canonica Orientale, Fonti, Serie I, 13 vols., Serie II, 16 vols., Series III, 3 vols. in 4, Cittá del Vaticano, Tipografia Polyglotta Vaticana, 1930- .

Collectanea in Usum Secretariae Sacrae Congregationis Episcoporum et Regularium cura A. Bizzarri Archiepiscopi Philippensis Secretarii edita, Romae: Ex Typographia Polyglotta, S. C. de Propaganda Fide, 1885.

Collectanea S. Congregationis de Propaganda Fide, 2 vols., Romae: Typographia Polyglotta, S. C. de Propaganda Fide, 1907.

Concilii Plenarii Baltimorensis II, in Ecclesia Metropolitana Baltimorensi a die VII ad diem XXI Octobris, A. D. MDCCCLXVI, Habiti, et a Sede Apostolica Recogniti, Acta et Decreta, Baltimorae, 1868.

Constitutiones Synodorum Dioecesanarum Sanctae Fidei Novi Mexici Primae, Secundae et Tertiae Quae Habitae fuerunt, Las Vegas, 1893.

Corpus Iuris Canonici, editio Lipsiensis secunda, post Aemilii Richteri curas instruxit Aemilius Friedberg, 2 vols., Lipsiae, 1879-1881.

Decreta Authentica Congregationis Sacrorum Rituum ex actis eiusdem collecta eiusque auctoritate promulgata sub auctoritate SS. Domini nostri Leonis Papae XIII, 6 vols., Romae: Ex Typographia Polyglotta S. C. de Prop. Fide, 1898-1927.

Decreta Synodorum Hartfordiensium in unum volumen collecta, Hartfordiae, 1902.

Dioecesana Synodus Firmana, Firmi, 1845.

Lucanae Ecclesiae Synodus Dioecesana, Lucae, 1887.

Mansi, Ioannes, *Sacrorum Conciliorum Nova et Amplissima Collectio,* 53 vols. in 60, Paris-Leipzig-Arnhem, 1901-1927.

Monumenta Germaniae Historica, Legum Sectio III, *Concilia,* Tom. II, Pars II, ed. A. Werminghoff, Hannoverae et Lipsiae, 1908.

Pallottini, Salvator, *Collectio Omnium Conclusionum et Resolutionum quae in causis propositis apud Sacram Congregationem Cardinalium S. Concilii Tridentini Interpretum prodierunt ab eius institutione anno MDLXIV ad annum MDCCCLX, distinctis titulis alphabetico ordine per materias digesta,* 17 vols., Romae, 1868-1893.

Rituale Romanum Pauli V Pont. Max. Iussu Editum, Romae: Typis Sac. Cong. de Prop. Fide, 1658.

Schroeder, Henry J., *Canons and Decrees of the Council of Trent: Original Text with English Translation,* St. Louis: B. Herder Book Co., 1941.

Statuta Dioeceseos Pittsburgensis in Synodis Dioecesanis, Habitis Annis Domini 1844, 1846, 1856, 1858, 1869, lata et prout nunc prostant promulgata in Synodo Dioecesana Sexta, Diebus 7, 8 et 9 Februarii 1893 Habita, Pittsburg, 1893.

Statuta Dioeceseos Trentonensis Quae in Synodo Dioecesana Secunda die Vigesima Quinta mensis Junii A. D. 1896 in Ecclesia Cathedrali Beatae Mariae Virgini Dicata Trentonii Habita, Trentonii, 1897.

Synodus Dioecesana Albanensis Tertia Quae Antecedentium etiam Complectitur Constitutiones, Diebus VI et VII Februarii A. D. 1884 in Seminario S. Josephi Habita, New York, 1884.

Synodus Dioecesana Chicagiensis Prima, Juxta Normam a Conc. Balt. III Praestitutam, Habita in Ecclesia Metropolitana S. S. Nominis, Chicagiae, 1887.

Synodus Dioecesana Ferrariensis, Ferrariae, 1781.

Synodus Dioecesana Neo-Eboracensis Quarta Quae Antecedentium etiam Complectitur Constitutiones, Diebus VIII et IX Nov. A. D. 1882, in Ecclesia Metropolitana S. Patritii, Neo-Eboraci Habita, Neo-Eboraci, 1882.

Synodus Dioecesana Syracusana Prima Die XIV Sept. A. D. 1887, in Ecclesia Sanctae Mariae in Coelos Assumptae Syracusis Habita, New York, 1887.

Synodus Dioecesana Wheelingensis Quarta Quae antecedentium etiam Complectitur Constitutiones Diebus 9 et 10 Aug. A. D. 1882 Habita, Wheelingii, 1882.

Thesaurus Resolutionum Sacrae Congregationis Concilii, 167 vols., Romae, 1718-1908.

Authors

Barbosa, Augustinus, *Pastoralis Solicitudinis sive de Officio et Potestate Episcopi Tripartita Descriptio*, Lugduni, 1628.

———, *Pastoralis Solicitudinis sive de Officio et Potestate Parochi Tripartita Descriptio*, Lugduni, 1655.

Bastien, P., *Directoire Canonique à L'Usage des Congregations à Voeux Simples*, Abbaye de Maredsous, 1904.

Batiffol, Pierre, *Etudes d'Histoire et de Théologie Positive*, Paris: V. Lecoffre, 1902.

Benedicti XIV Omnia Opera, 17 vols. in 18, Prati, 1829-1847.

———, *Pont. Opt. Max. olim Prosperi Card. de Lambertinis Institutiones Ecclesiasticae*, 12 vols., Romae, 1747-1751.

Berutti, C., *Institutiones Iuris Canonici*, 6 vols., Vol. III, Taurini-Romae: Marietti, 1936.

Blat, A., *Commentarium Textus Codicis Iuris Canonici*, 5 vols. in 7, Romae: Ex Typographia Pontificia in Instituto Pii IX, 1921-1938. Lib. I, 1921; Lib. II, ed. altera, 1921; Lib. II, partes II, III, 3. ed., 1938; Lib. III, Pars I, 2. ed. aucta et emendata, 1924; Lib. III, partes II-VI, 2. ed. examinata denuo et aucta, 1934; Lib. IV, 1927; Lib. V, 1924.

Cappello, Felix M., *Tractatus Canonico-Moralis de Sacramentis*, 3 vols. in 6, Vol. II, *De Poenitentia*, 3. ed., Taurinorum Augustae: Marietti, 1938.

Catalani, Iosephus, *Rituale Romanum Benedicti Papae XIV iussu editum*, Patavii, 1760.

Cerato, P., *De Delicto Sollicitationis*, Patavii: Typis Seminarii, 1922.

Chelodi, Ioannes, *Ius Canonicum de Personis*, 3. ed. curavit Pius Ciprotti, Trento: Libreria Moderna Editrice, 1942.

Cocchi, Guidus, *Commentarium in Codicem Iuris Canonici ad Usum Scholarum*, 8 vols. in 5, Vol. IV, 3. ed., 1932, Taurinorum Augustae: Marietti, 1932.

Coronata, Matthaeus Conte A., *De Locis et Temporibus Sacris*, Augustae Taurinorum: Marietti, 1922.

———, *Institutiones Iuris Canonici ad usum utriusque cleri et scholarum De Sacramentis Tractatus Canonicus*, 3 vols., Taurini-Romae: Marietti, 1943-1946.

———, *Institutiones Iuris Canonici*, 2. ed., 5 vols., Taurini: Marietti, 1939-1947.

De Bonis, Joseph, *De Oratoriis Publicis Tractatus Historico-Canonicus*, Mediolani, 1761.

De Meester, Alphonsus, *Iuris Canonici et Iuris Canonico-Civilis Compendium*, ed. nova, 3 vols. in 4, Vol. II, Brugis: Desclée, De Brouwer, et Soc. 1923.

Dictionnaire de Droit Canonique, Paris: Librairie Letouzey et Ané, 1924- .

Fanfani, L., *De Iure Religiosorum ad Normam Codicis Iuris Canonici*, ed. altera, Taurini-Romae: Ex Officina Libraria Marietti, 1925.

Ferraris, Lucius, *Prompta Bibliotheca Canonica, Iuridica, Moralis, Theologica necnon Ascetica, Polemica, Rubricistica, Historica*, 9 vols., Romae, 1885-1899.

Ferreres, Ioannes, *Institutiones Canonicae iuxta novissimum codicem Pii X a Benedicto XV promulgatum iuxtaque praescripta Hispanae disciplinae et Americae Latinae*, 2 vols., ed. altera, Barcinone, 1920.

Forcellini, Aegidius, *Lexicon Totius Latinitatis*, 6 vols., Patavii: Typis Seminarii, 1940.

Formisano, Giuseppe, *Commentario sulla Costituzione Apostolicae Sedis*, 6. ed., Napoli, 1876.

Giraldi, U., *Expositio Iuris Pontificii iuxta recentiorem ecclesiae disciplinam in duas partes distributa*, 2 vols., Romae, 1769.

Leitner, M., *Handbuch des katholischen Kirchenrechts auf Grund des neuen Kodex*, 2 vols., Regensburg: Friederich Pustet, 1919-1927.

Martène, Edmundus, *Tractatus de Antiquis Ecclesiae Ritibus Libri Quatuor*, 3 vols., Rotomagi: G. Behourt, 1700-1702.

Maschat, Remigius, *Institutiones Canonicae*, 4 vols. in 2, Florentiae, 1854.

Maupied, Franciscus L. M., *Iuris Canonici Compendium*, 2 vols., Parisiis, 1863.

McCormick, R., *Confessors of Religious*, The Catholic University of America Canon Law Studies, n. 33, Washington, D. C.: The Catholic University of America, 1926.

Medina, Ioannes, *De Paenitentia, Restitutione et Contractibus*, Ingolstadii, 1681.

Migne, Jacques Paul, *Patrologiae Cursus Completus, Series Latina*, 221 vols., Parisiis, 1844-1864.

———, *Theologiae Cursus Completus*, 28 vols., Parisiis, 1839-1845.

Morin, Jean, *Commentarius Historicus de Disciplina in Administratione Sacramenti Poenitentiae*, Venetiis: N. Pezzana, 1702.

Pellizzari, Franciscus, *Tractatio de Monialibus*, ed. tertia, Venetiis, 1651.

Pignatelli, Iacobus, *Consultationes Canonicae*, 11 vols. in 5, Coloniae Allobrogum, 1700.

Pilatus, Leopold von, *Origines Iuris Pontificii ad Carolum Sextum*, Tridenti, 1739.

Prümmer, D. M., *Manuale Iuris Canonici in Usum Scholarum*, 4. et 5. ed., Friburgi Brisgoviae: B. Herder and Company, 1927.

Raus, J. B., *Institutiones Canonicae iuxta Novum Codicem Iuris pro Scholis vel ad Usum Privatum synthetice Redactae,* 2. ed., Lugduni-Parisiis: Typis Emmanuelis Vitte, 1931.

Regatillo, Eduardus, *Institutiones Iuris Canonici,* 2 vols., Vol. II, *De Rebus,* Santander: Sal Terrae, 1942.

———, *Ius Sacramentarium,* 2 vols., Vol. I, Santander: Sal Terrae, 1945.

Reilly, Thomas F., *The Visitation of Religious,* The Catholic University of America Canon Law Studies, n. 112, Washington, D. C.: The Catholic University of America, 1938.

Romani, Sylvius, *Institutiones Iuris Canonici,* 2 vols. in 3, Vol. II, *Ius Administrativum de Sacramentis,* Pars Prior, Romae: Editrice "Iustitia," 1944.

Rota, Petrus, *Enchiridion Confessarii et Iudicis Ecclesiastici seu Ratio Compendiosa iudicandi in utroque foro de abusu sacramenti poenitentiae et oeconomice procedendi in caeteris clericorum causis disciplinaribus et criminalibus,* Augustae Taurinorum, 1884.

Sartori, Cosmas, *Enchiridion Canonicum seu Sanctae Sedis Responsiones post Editum Codicem I. C. Datae iuxta Canonum Codicis Ordinem Digestae Notulisque Ordinatae,* 8. ed., Romae: Pontificium Athenaeum Antonianum, 1947.

Schaefer, Timotheus, *De Religiosis ad Normam Codicis Iuris Canonici,* 3. ed., Romae: Typis Polyglottis Vaticanis, 1940.

Snee, Joseph-Clark, J. Donald, *Diocesan Faculties in the United States,* Woodstock: Woodstock College Press, 1948.

Sipos, Stephanus, *Enchiridion Iuris Canonici,* 3. ed., Pécs: Ex Typographia "Haladás R. T., " 1936.

Sobradillo, A. M., *Tractatus de Religiosarum Confessariis ad Normam Codicis Iuris Canonici Concinnatus,* Taurini: Berutti, 1932.

Thurston, Herbert, *Lent and Holy Week,* New York: Longmans, Green and Co., 1904.

Toso, Albertus, *Ad Codicem Iuris Canonici Benedicti XV Pont. Max. Auctoritate Promulgatum Commentaria Minora,* 5 vols., Romae: Ius Pontificium, 1918-1927.

Van der Stappen, J. F., *Sacra Liturgia,* 5 vols., Vol. IV, Mechliniae, 1900.

Vermeersch, A., *De Religiosis Institutis et Personis Tractatus Canonico-Moralis,* 2 vols., Vol. II, 4. ed., Brugis, 1909.

Vermeersch, A.-Creusen, J., *Epitome Iuris Canonici,* 6. ed., 3 vols., Mechliniae-Romae: Dessain, 6. ed., 1937-1946.

Villien, A., *The History and Liturgy of the Sacraments,* English translation by H. W. Edwards, London: Burns, Oates and Washbourne Ltd., 1932.

Wigandt, Martin, *Tribunal Confessariorum et Ordinandorum,* Venetiis, 1717.

ARTICLES

André, J., "Medieval Confessionals in England," *Reliquary,* XXIV (1883-1884), 129-132.

Anonymous, "Confession of Women outside the Confessional," *The Ecclesiastical Review,* XC (1934), 159-161.

———, "Is [a] Confessional Required for Valid Confession of Women?" *The Ecclesiastical Review,* CII (1940), 532-533.

———, "Pontificiae Commissionis Codici Interpretando Praepositae Responsiones Authenticae," *Jus Pontificium,* III (1923), 118-119.

Barraud, L., "Notice sur les Confessionaux," *Bulletin Monumental,* XXXIV (1868), 695-755, 825-847.

Cochet, J., "Lettre sur les confessionaux au moyen-age," *Bulletin Monumental,* XXXVII (1871), 51-57.

Creusen, Joseph, "Confesseur Occasionnel des Religieuses," *Nouvelle Revue Théologique,* LXII (1935), 512-514.

———, "Confesseurs des Religieuses," *Nouvelle Revue Théologique,* LV (1928), 766-767.

———, "Confessions of Religious Women," *The Ecclesiastical Review,* LXXIV (1926), 506-509.

———, "Les Dernières Réponses de la Commission d'Interprétation du Code," *Nouvelle Revue Théologique,* LV (1928), 276-295.

Fallon, M., "Canon 522 and Confession of a Nun in a Sacristy," *The Irish Ecclesiastical Record,* 5. series, XLIX (1937), 311-315.

Goyeneche, S., "Consultationes," *Commentarium pro Religiosis,* III (1922), 335-336.

———, "De Confessione Religiosarum," *Apollinaris,* VIII (1935), 556-557.

———, "De vi can. 522," *Commentarium pro Religiosis,* II (1921), 13-24.

Jombart, E., "Confessional," *Dictionnaire de Droit Canonique,* XIX (1944), 64-66.

Larraona, A., "Commentarium Codicis," *Commentarium pro Religiosis,* VIII (1927), 440-448.

Mahoney, E., "Confessions of Religious Women in Exceptional Cases," *The Ecclesiastical Review,* LXXIV (1926), 24-44.

Maroto, P., "Annotationes ad III Responsum," *Commentarium pro Religiosis,* II (1921), 36-38.

———, "De Loco ad Confessiones Excipiendas," *Apollinaris,* I (1928), 407-411.

———, "Pontificia Commissio ad Codicis Canones Authentice Interpretandos," *Commentarium pro Religiosis,* IX (1928), 93-97.

Vermeersch, A., "De Confessionum regimine apud religiosos et religiosas," *Periodica,* IX (1921), (9)-(16).

———, "Interpretatio can. 19 de stricta quarundam legum interpretatione cum nonnullis applicationibus," *Periodica,* XI (1922), (8)-(15).

———, "Moralis et Pastoralis Consideratio de Religiosarum Confessione Facta Confessario ex can. 522," *Periodica,* XI (1922), (1)-(8).

Vromant, G., "De Regimine Paroeciarum et Quasi-Paroeciarum Religiosis Sodalibus Concreditarum," *Jus Pontificium,* XIII (1933), 274-284.

Woywod, Stanislaus, "Sacramental Confession of Sisters," *The Homiletic and Pastoral Review,* XXXVI (1936), 870-872.

PERIODICALS

American Ecclesiastical Review, The, Vols. I-XXXII, Philadelphia, 1889-1905; *The Ecclesiastical Review,* Vols. XXXIII-CIX, Philadelphia, 1905-1943; *The American Ecclesiastical Review,* Washington, D. C., Vol. CX, 1944- .

Analecta Ecclesiastica, Romae, 1893-1911.

Apollinaris, Romae, 1928- .

Bulletin Monumental, Paris, 1834-1896.

Commentarium pro Religiosis, Romae, 1920-1934; *Commentarium pro Religiosis et Missionariis,* Romae, 1935- .

Homiletic and Pastoral Review, The, New York, 1900- .

Irish Ecclesiastical Record, The, Dublin, 1864- .

Jus Pontificium, Romae, 1921-1940.

Nouvelle Revue Théologique, Tournai, 1869- .

Periodica de Religiosis et Missionariis, Brugis, 1905-1919; *Periodica de Re Canonica et Morali utilia praesertim Religiosis et Missionariis,* Brugis, 1920-1927; *Periodica de Re Morali, Canonica, Liturgica,* Brugis (1927-1936) et Romae (1937-).

Reliquary, London, 1860-1909.

ABBREVIATIONS

AAS — *Acta Apostolicae Sedis.*

AER — *The American Ecclesiastical Review.*

ER — *The Ecclesiastical Review.*

Fontes — *Codicis Iuris Canonici Fontes.*

Fonti — *Codificazione Canonica Orientale.*

Mansi — *Sacrorum Conciliorum Nova et Amplissima Collectio.*

Periodica — *Periodica de Re Canonica, Morali, Liturgica.*

S. C. C. — Sacra Congregatio Concilii.

S. C. de Prop. Fide — Sacra Congregatio de Propaganda Fide.

S. C. de Rel. — Sacra Congregatio de Religiosis.

S. C. Ep. et Reg. — Sacra Congregatio Episcoporum et Regularium.

S. C. S. Off. — Sacra Congregatio Sancti Officii.

S. R. C. — Sacra Rituum Congregatio.

Thesaurus — *Thesaurus Resolutionum Sacrae Congregationis Concilii.*

BIOGRAPHICAL NOTE

Francis J. Fazzalaro was born in Meriden, Connecticut, on June 14, 1919. After completing his elementary studies there, he graduated from Meriden High School in 1937. He then attended St. Thomas' Preparatory Seminary in Bloomfield, Connecticut, finishing his course of studies in 1939. That same year he entered St. Bernard's Seminary, Rochester, New York, where he completed his studies in philosophy and theology, receiving the degree of Bachelor of Arts in 1941. He was ordained to the Priesthood on March 17, 1945. After a year and a half of parochial work in St. Anthony's Church, Hartford, Connecticut, he enrolled in the School of Canon Law at The Catholic University of America in October, 1946. He received the Baccalaureate Degree in Canon Law in June, 1947, and the Licentiate Degree in June, 1948.

ALPHABETICAL INDEX

CANON LAW STUDIES *

1. Freriks, Rev. Celestine A., C. PP. S., J. C. D., Religious Congregations in Their External Relations, 121 pp., 1916.
2. Galliher, Rev. Daniel M., O. P., J. C. D., Canonical Elections, 117 pp., 1917.
3. Borkowski, Rev. Aurelius L., O. F. M., J. C. D., De Confraternitatibus Ecclesiasticis, 136 pp., 1918.
4. Castillo, Rev. Cayo, J. C. D., Disertación Historico-Canonica sobre la Potestad del Cabildo en Sede Vacante o Impedida del Vicario Capitular, 99 pp., 1919 (1918).
5. Kubelbeck, Rev. William J., S. T. B., J. C. D., The Sacred Penitentiaria and Its Relation to Faculties of Ordinaries and Priests, 129 pp., 1918.
6. Petrovits, Rev. Joseph, J. C., S. T. D., J. C. D., The New Church Law on Matrimony, X-461 pp., 1919.
7. Hickey, Rev. John J., S. T. B., J. C. D., Irregularities and Simple Impediments in the New Code of Canon Law, 100 pp., 1920.
8. Klekotka, Rev. Peter J., S. T. B., J. C. D., Diocesan Consultors, 179 pp., 1920.
9. Wanenmacher, Rev. Francis, J. C. D., The Evidence in Ecclesiastical Procedure Affecting the Marriage Bond, 1920 (Printed 1935).
10. Golden, Rev. Henry Francis, J. C. D., Parochial Benefices in the New Code, IV-119 pp., 1921 (Printed 1925).
11. Koudelka, Rev. Charles J., J. C. D., Pastors, Their Rights and Duties According to the New Code of Canon Law, 211 pp., 1921.
12. Melo, Rev. Antonius, O. F. M., J. C. D., De Exemptione Regularium, X-188 pp., 1921.
13. Schaaf, Rev. Valentine Theodore, O. F. M., S. T. B., J. C. D., The Cloister, X-180 pp., 1921.
14. Burke, Rev. Thomas Joseph, S. T. D., J. C. D., Competence in Ecclesiastical Tribunals, IV-117 pp., 1922.
15. Leech, Rev. George Leo, J. C. D., A Comparative Study of the Constitution "Apostolicae Sedis" and the "Codex Juris Canonici," 179 pp., 1922.
16. Motry, Rev. Hubert Louis, S. T. D., J. C. D., Diocesan Faculties According to the Code of Canon Law, II-167 pp., 1922.
17. Murphy, Rev. George Lawrence, J. C. D., Delinquencies and Penalties in the Administration and the Reception of the Sacraments, IV-121 pp., 1923.
18. O'Reilly, Rev. John Anthony, S. T. B., J. C. D., Ecclesiastical Sepulture in the New Code of Canon Law, II-129 pp., 1923.

*All published numbers are available from the Catholic University of America Press, 620 Michigan Ave., N. E., Washington, D. C., except the following: nos. 1-114 inclusive, 116, 118, 120, 121, 122, 123, 136, 153, 162, 182 and 198. But the following numbers, now reissued, are obtainable from *The Jurist*, The Catholic University of America, Washington 17, D. C., namely: nos. 5, 7, 11, 17, 18, 19, 26, 28, 30, 31, 34, 42, 44, 51, 52 and 61.

19. MICHALICKA, REV. WENCESLAS CYRILL, O. S. B., J. C. D., Judicial Procedure in Dismissal of Clerical Exempt Religious, 107 pp., 1923.
20. DARGIN, REV. EDWARD VINCENT, S. T. B., J. C. D., Reserved Cases According to the Code of Canon Law, IV-103 pp., 1924.
21. GODFREY, REV. JOHN A., S. T. B., J. C. D., The Right of Patronage According to the Code of Canon Law, 153 pp., 1924.
22. HAGEDORN, REV. FRANCIS EDWARD, J. C. D., General Legislation on Indulgences, II-154 pp., 1924.
23. KING, REV. JAMES IGNATIUS, J. C. D., The Administration of the Sacraments to Dying Non-Catholics, V-141 pp., 1924.
24. WINSLOW, REV. FRANCIS JOSEPH, O. F. M., J. C. D., Vicars and Prefects Apostolic, IV-149 pp., 1924.
25. CORREA, REV. JOSE SERVELION, S. T. L., J. C. D., La Potestad Legislativa de la Iglesia Catolica, IV-127 pp., 1925.
26. DUGAN, REV. HENRY FRANCIS, A. M., J. C. D., The Judiciary Department of the Diocesan Curia, 87 pp., 1925.
27. KELLER, REV. CHARLES FREDERICK, S. T. B., J. C. D., Mass Stipends, 167 pp., 1925.
28. PASCHANG, REV. JOHN LINUS, J. C. D., The Sacramentals According to the Code of Canon Law, 129 pp., 1925.
29. PIONTEK, REV. CYRILLUS, O. F. M., S. T. B., J. C. D., De Indulto Exclaustrationis necnon Saecularizationis, XIII-289 pp., 1925.
30. KEARNEY, REV. RICHARD JOSEPH, S. T. B., J. C. D., Sponsors at Baptism According to the Code of Canon Law, IV-127 pp., 1925.
31. BARTLETT, REV. CHESTER JOSEPH, A. M., LL. B., J. C. D., The Tenure of Parochial Property in the United States of America, V-108 pp., 1926.
32. KILKER, REV. ADRIAN JEROME, J. C. D., Extreme Unction, V-425 pp., 1926.
33. MCCORMICK, REV. ROBERT EMMETT, J. C. D., Confessors of Religious, VIII-266 pp., 1926.
34. MILLER, REV. NEWTON THOMAS, J. C. D., Founded Masses According to the Code of Canon Law, VII-93 pp., 1926.
35. ROELKER, REV. EDWARD G., S. T. D., J. C. D., Principles of Privilege According to the Code of Canon Law, XI-166 pp., 1926.
36. BAKALARCZYK, REV. RICHARDUS, M. I. C., J. U. D., De Novitiatu, VIII-208 pp., 1927.
37. PIZZUTI, REV. LAWRENCE, O. F. M., J. U. L., De Parochis Religiosis, 1927 (Not Printed).
38. BLILEY, REV. NICHOLAS MARTIN, O. S. B., J. C. D., Altars According to the Code of Canon Law, XIX-132 pp., 1927.
39. BROWN, MR. BRENDAN FRANCIS, A. B., LL. M., J. U. D., The Canonical Juristic Personality with Special References to its Status in the United States of America, V-212 pp., 1927.

40. CAVANAUGH, REV. WILLIAM THOMAS, C. P., J. U. D., The Reservation of the Blessed Sacrament, VIII-101 pp., 1927.
41. DOHENY, REV. WILLIAM J., C. S. C., A. B., J. U. D., Church Property: Modes of Acquisition, X-118 pp., 1927.
42. FELDHAUS, REV. ALOYSIUS H., C. PP. S., J. C. D., Oratories, IX-141 pp., 1927.
43. KELLY, REV. JAMES PATRICK, A. B., J. C. D., The Jurisdiction of the Simple Confessor, X-208 pp., 1927.
44. NEUBERGER, REV. NICHOLAS J., J. C. D., Canon 6 or the Relation of the Codex Juris Canonici to the Preceding Legislation, V-95 pp., 1927.
45. O'KEEFE, REV. GERALD MICHAEL, J. C. D., Matrimonial Dispensations, Powers of Bishops, Priests, and Confessors, VIII-232 pp., 1927.
46. QUIGLEY, REV. JOSEPH A. M., A. B., J. C. D., Condemned Societies, 139 pp., 1927.
47. ZAPLOTNIK, REV. JOHANNES LEO, J. C. D., De Vicariis Foraneis, X-142 pp., 1927.
48. DUSKIE, REV. JOHN ALOYSIUS, A. B., J. C. D., The Canonical Status of the Orientals in the United States, VIII-196 pp., 1928.
49. HYLAND, REV. FRANCIS EDWARD, J. C. D., Excommunication, Its Nature, Historical Development and Effects, VIII-181 pp., 1928.
50. REINMANN, REV. GERALD JOSEPH, O. M. C., J. C. D., The Third Order Secular of Saint Francis, 201 pp., 1928.
51. SCHENK, REV. FRANCIS J., J. C. D., The Matrimonial Impediments of Mixed Religion and Disparity of Cult, XVI-318 pp., 1929.
52. COADY, REV. JOHN JOSEPH, S. T. D., J. U. D., A. M., The Appointment of Pastors, VIII-150 pp., 1929.
53. KAY, REV. THOMAS HENRY, J. C. D., Competence in Matrimonial Procedure, VIII-164 pp., 1929.
54. TURNER, REV. SIDNEY JOSEPH, C. P., J. U. D., The Vow of Poverty, XLIX-217 pp., 1929.
55. KEARNEY, REV. RAYMOND A., A. B., S. T. D., J. C. D., The Principles of Delegation, VII-149 pp., 1929.
56. CONRAN, REV. EDWARD JAMES, A. B., J. C. D., The Interdict, V-163 pp., 1930.
57. O'NEILL, REV. WILLIAM H., J. C. D., Papal Rescripts of Favor, VII-218 pp., 1930.
58. BASTNAGEL, REV. CLEMENT VINCENT, J. U. D., The Appointment of Parochial Adjutants and Assistants, XV-257 pp., 1930.
59. FERRY, REV. WILLIAM A., A. B., J. C. D., Stole Fees, V-136 pp., 1930.
60. COSTELLO, REV. JOHN MICHAEL, A. B., J. C. D., Domicile and Quasi-Domicile, VII-201 pp., 1930.
61. KREMER, REV. MICHAEL NICHOLAS, A. B., S. T. B., J. C. D., Church Support in the United States, VI-136 pp., 1930.

62. ANGULO, REV. LUIS, C. M., J. C. D., Legislación de la Iglesia sobre la intención en la applicación de la Santa Misa, VII-104 pp., 1931.
63. FREY, REV. WOLFGANG NORBERT, O. S. B., A. B., J. C. D., The Act of Religious Profession, VIII-174 pp., 1931.
64. ROBERTS, REV. JAMES BRENDAN, A. B., J. C. D., The Banns of Marriage, XIV-140 pp., 1931.
65. RYDER, REV. RAYMOND ALOYSIUS, A. B., J. C. D., Simony, IX-151 pp., 1931.
66. CAMPAGNA, REV. ANGELO, PH. D., J. U. D., Il Vicario Generale del Vescovo, VII-205 pp., 1931.
67. COX, REV. JOSEPH GODFREY, A. B., J. C. D., The Administration of Seminaries, VI-124 pp., 1931.
68. GREGORY, REV. DONALD J., J. U. D., The Pauline Privilege, XV-165 pp., 1931.
69. DONOHUE, REV. JOHN F., J. C. D., The Impediment of Crime, VII-110 pp., 1931.
70. DOOLEY, REV. EUGENE A., O. M. I., J. C. D., Church Law on Sacred Relics, IX-143 pp., 1931.
71. ORTH, REV. CLEMENT RAYMOND, O. M. C., J. C. D., The Approbation of Religious Institutes, 171 pp., 1931.
72. PERNICONE, REV. JOSEPH M., A. B., J. C. D., The Ecclesiastical Prohibition of Books, XII-267 pp., 1932.
73. CLINTON, REV. CONNELL, A. B., J. C. D., The Paschal Precept, IX-108 pp., 1932.
74. DONNELLY, REV. FRANCIS B., A. M., S. T. L., J. C. D., The Diocesan Synod, VIII-125 pp., 1932.
75. TORRENTE, REV. CAMILO, C. M. F., J. C. D., Las Procesiones Sagradas, V-145 pp., 1932.
76. MURPHY, REV. EDWIN J., C. PP. S., J. C. D., Suspension Ex Informata Conscientia, XI-122 pp., 1932.
77. MACKENZIE, REV. ERIC F., A. M., S. T. L., J. C. D., The Delict of Heresy in its Commission, Penalization, Absolution, VII-124 pp., 1932.
78. LYONS, REV. AVITUS E., S. T. B., J. C. D., The Collegiate Tribunal of First Instance, XI-147 pp., 1932.
79. CONNOLLY, REV. THOMAS A., J. C. D., Appeals, XI-195 pp., 1932.
80. SANGMEISTER, REV. JOSEPH V., A. B., J. C. D., Force and Fear as Precluding Matrimonial Consent, V-211 pp., 1932.
81. JAEGER, REV. LEO A., A. B., J. C. D., The Administration of Vacant and Quasi-Vacant Episcopal Sees in the United States, IX-229 pp., 1932.
82. RIMLINGER, REV. HERBERT T., J. C. D., Error Invalidating Matrimonial Consent, VII-79 pp., 1932.
83. BARRETT, REV. JOHN D. M., S. S., J. C. D., A Comparative Study of the Councils of Baltimore and the Code of Canon Law, IX-223 pp., 1932.

84. Carberry, Rev. John J., Ph. D., S. T. D., J. C. D., The Juridical Form of Marriage, X-177 pp., 1934.
85. Dolan, Rev. John L., A. B., J. C. D., The Defensor Vinculi, XII-157 pp., 1934.
86. Hannan, Rev. Jerome D., A. M., S. T. D., LL. B., J. C. D., The Canon Law of Wills, IX-517 pp., 1934.
87. Lemieux, Rev. Delise A., A. M., J. C. D., The Sentence in Ecclesiastical Procedure, IX-131 pp., 1934.
88. O'Rourke, Rev. James J., A. B., J. C. D., Parish Registers, VII-109 pp., 1934.
89. Timlin, Rev. Bartholomew, O. F. M., A. M., J. C. D., Conditional Matrimonial Consent, X-381 pp., 1934.
90. Wahl, Rev. Francis X., A. B., J. C. D., The Matrimonial Impediments of Consanguinity and Affinity, VI-125 pp., 1934.
91. White, Rev. Robert J., A. B., LL. B., S. T. B., J. C. D., Canonical Ante-Nuptial Promises and the Civil Law, VI-152 pp., 1934.
92. Herrera, Rev. Antonio Parra, O. C. D., J. C. D., Legislación Eclesiástica sobra el Ayuno y la Abstinencia, XI-191 pp., 1935.
93. Kennedy, Rev. Edwin J., J. C. D., The Special Matrimonial Process in Cases of Evident Nullity, X-165 pp., 1935.
94. Manning, Rev. John J., A. B., J. C. D., Presumption of Law in Matrimonial Procedure, XI-111 pp., 1935.
95. Moeder, Rev. John M., J. C. D., The Proper Bishop for Ordination and Dimissorial Letters, VII-135 pp., 1935.
96. O'Mara, Rev. William A., A. B., J. C. D., Canonical Causes for Matrimonial Dispensations, IX-155 pp., 1935.
97. Reilly, Rev. Peter, J. C. D., Residence of Pastors, IX-81 pp., 1935.
98. Smith, Rev. Mariner T., O. P., S. T. Lr., J. C. D., The Penal Law for Religious, VIII-169 pp., 1935.
99. Whalen, Rev. Donald W., A. M., J. C. D., The Value of Testimonial Evidence in Matrimonial Procedure, XIII-297 pp., 1935.
100. Cleary, Rev. Joseph F., J. C. D., Canonical Limitations on the Alienation of Church Property, VIII-141 pp., 1936.
101. Glynn, Rev. John C., J. C. D., The Promoter of Justice, XX-337 pp., 1936.
102. Brennan, Rev. James H., S. S., M. A., S. T. B., J. C. D., The Simple Convalidation of Marriage, VI-135 pp., 1937.
103. Brunini, Rev. Joseph Bernard, J. C. D., The Clerical Obligations of Canons 139 and 142, X-121 pp., 1937.
104. Connor, Rev. Maurice, A. B., J. C. D., The Administrative Removal of Pastors, VIII-159 pp., 1937.
105. Guilfoyle, Rev. Merlin Joseph, J. C. D., Custom, XI-144 pp., 1937.
106. Hughes, Rev. James Austin, A. B., A. M., J. C. D., Witnesses in Criminal Trials of Clerics, IX-140 pp., 1937.

107. JANSEN, REV. RAYMOND J., A. B., S. T. L., J. C. D., Canonical Provisions for Catechetical Instruction, VII-153 pp., 1937.

108. KEALY, REV. JOHN JAMES, A. B., J. C. D., The Introductory Libellus in Church Court Procedure, XI-121 pp., 1937.

109. MCMANUS, REV. JAMES EDWARD, C. SS. R., J. C. D., The Administration of Temporal Goods in Religious Institutes, XVI-196 pp., 1937.

110. MORIARTY, REV. EUGENE JAMES, J. C. D., Oaths in Ecclesiastical Courts, X-115 pp., 1937.

111. RAINER, REV. ELIGIUS GEORGE, C. SS. R., J. C. D., Suspension of Clerics, XVII-249 pp., 1937.

112. REILLY, REV. THOMAS F., C. SS. R., J. C. D., Visitation of Religious, VI-195 pp., 1938.

113. MORIARTY, REV. FRANCIS E., C. SS. R., J. C. D., The Extraordinary Absolution from Censures, XV-334 pp., 1938.

114. CONNOLLY, REV. NICHOLAS P., J. C. D., The Canonical Erection of Parishes, X-132 pp., 1938.

115. DONOVAN, REV. JAMES JOSEPH, J. C. D., The Pastor's Obligation in Prenuptial Investigation, XII-322 pp., 1938.

116. HARRIGAN, REV. ROBERT J., M. A., S. T. B., J. C. D., The Radical Sanation of Invalid Marriages, VIII-208 pp., 1938.

117. BOFFA, REV. CONRAD HUMBERT, J. C. D., Canonical Provisions for Catholic Schools, VII-211 pp., 1939.

118. PARSONS, REV. ANSCAR JOHN, O. M. CAP., J. C. D., Canonical Elections, XII-236 pp., 1939.

119. REILLY, REV. EDWARD MICHAEL, A. B., J. C. D., The General Norms of Dispensation, XII-156 pp., 1939.

120. RYAN, REV. GERALD ALOYSIUS, A. B., J. C. D., Principles of Episcopal Jurisdiction, XII-172 pp., 1939.

121. BURTON, REV. FRANCIS JAMES, C. S. C., A. B., J. C. D., A Commentary on Canon 1125, X-222 pp., 1940.

122. MIASKIEWICZ, REV. FRANCIS SIGISMUND, J. C. D., Supplied Jurisdiction According to Canon 209, XII-340 pp., 1940.

123. RICE, REV. PATRICK WILLIAM, A. B., J. C. D., Proof of Death in Prenuptial Investigation, VIII-156 pp., 1940.

124. ANGLIN, REV. THOMAS FRANCIS, M. S., J. C. D., The Eucharistic Fast, VIII-183 pp., 1941.

125. COLEMAN, REV. JOHN JEROME, J. C. D., The Minister of Confirmation, VI-153 pp., 1941.

126. DOWNS, REV. JOHN EMMANUEL, A. B., J. C. D., The Concept of Clerical Immunity, XI-163 pp., 1941.

127. ESSWEIN, REV. ANTHONY ALBERT, J. C. D., Extrajudicial Penal Powers of Ecclesiastical Superiors, X-144 pp., 1941.

128. FARRELL, REV. BENJAMIN FRANCIS, M. A., S. T. L., J. C. D., The Rights and Duties of the Local Ordinary Regarding Congregations of Women Religious of Pontifical Approval, V-195 pp., 1941.
129. FEENEY, REV. THOMAS JOHN, A. B., S. T. L., J. C. D., Restitutio in Integrum, VI-169 pp., 1941.
130. FINDLAY, REV. STEPHEN WILLIAM, O. S. B., A. B., J. C. D., Canonical Norms Governing the Deposition and Degradation of Clerics, XVII-279 pp., 1941.
131. GOODWINE, REV. JOHN, A. B., S. T. L., J. C. D., The Right of the Church to Acquire Property, VIII-119 pp., 1941.
132. HESTON, REV. EDWARD LOUIS, C. S. C., PH. D., S. T. D., J. C. D., The Alienation of Church Property in the United States, XII-222 pp., 1941.
133. HOGAN, REV. JAMES JOHN, A. B., S. T. L., J. C. D., Judicial Advocates and Procurators, XIII-200 pp., 1941.
134. KEALY, REV. THOMAS M., A. B., LITT. B., J. C. D., Dowry of Women Religious, IX-152 pp., 1941.
135. KEENE, REV. MICHAEL JAMES, O. S. B., J. C. D., Religious Ordinaries and Canon 198, V-164 pp., 1941 (Printed 1942).
136. KERIN, REV. CHARLES A., S. S., M. A., S. T. B., J. C. D., The Privation of Christian Burial, XVI-279 pp., 1941.
137. LOUIS, REV. WILLIAM FRANCIS, M. A., J. C. D., Diocesan Archives, X-101 pp., 1941.
138. MCDEVITT, REV. GILBERT JOSEPH, A. B., J. C. D., Legitimacy and Legitimation, X-247 pp., 1941.
139. MCDONOUGH, REV. THOMAS JOSEPH, A. B., J. C. D., Apostolic Administrators, X-217 pp., 1941.
140. MEIER, REV. CARL ANTHONY, A. B., J. C. D., Penal Administrative Procedure Against Negligent Pastors, XI-240 pp., 1941.
141. SCHMIDT, REV. JOHN ROGG, A. B., J. C. D., The Principles of Authentic Interpretation in Canon 17 of the Code of Canon Law, XII-331 pp., 1941.
142. SLAFKOSKY, REV. ANDREW LEONARD, A. B., J. C. D., The Canonical Episcopal Visitation of the Diocese, X-197 pp., 1941.
143. SWOBODA, REV. INNOCENT ROBERT, O. F. M., J. C. D., Ignorance in Relation to the Imputability of Delicts, IX-271 pp., 1941.
144. DUBE, REV. ARTHUR JOSEPH, A. B., J. C. D., The General Principles for the Reckoning of Time in Canon Law, VIII-299 pp., 1941.
145. MCBRIDE, REV. JAMES T., A. B., J. C. D., Incardination and Excardination of Seculars, XX-585 pp., 1941.
146. KROL, REV. JOHN T., J. C. D., The Defendant in Ecclesiastical Trials, XII-207 pp., 1942.
147. COMYNS, REV. JOSEPH J., C. SS. R., A. B., J. C. D., Papal and Episcopal Administration of Church Property, XIV-155 pp., 1942.
148. BARRY, REV. GARRETT FRANCIS, O. M. I., J. C. D., Violation of the Cloister, XII-260 pp., 1942.

149. BOLDUC, REV. GATIEN, C. S. V., A. B., S. T. L., J. C. D., Les Etudes dans les Religions Cléricales, VIII-155 pp., 1942.
150. BOYLE, REV. DAVID JOHN, M. A., J. C. D., The Juridic Effects of Moral Certitude on Pre-Nuptial Guarantees, XII-188 pp., 1942.
151. CANAVAN, REV. WALTER JOSEPH, M. A., LITT. D., J. C. D., The Profession of Faith, XII-143 pp., 1942.
152. DESROCHERS, REV. BRUNO, A. B., PH. L., S. T. B., J. C. D., Le Premier Concile Plénier de Québec et le Code de Droit Canonique, XIV-186 pp., 1942.
153. DILLON, REV. ROBERT EDWARD, A. B., J. C. D., Common Law Marriage, X-148 pp., 1942.
154. DODWELL, REV. EDWARD JOHN, PH. D., S. T. B., J. C. D., The Time and Place for the Celebration of Marriage, X-156 pp., 1942.
155. DONNELLAN, REV. THOMAS ANDREW, A. B., J. C. D., The Obligation of the Missa pro Populo, VII-131 pp., 1942.
156. ELTZ, REV. LOUIS ANTHONY, A. B., J. C. D., Cooperation in Crime, XII-208 pp., 1942.
157. GASS, REV. SYLVESTER FRANCIS, M. A., J. C. D., Ecclesiastical Pensions, XI-206 pp., 1942.
158. GUINIVEN, REV. JOHN JOSEPH, C. SS. R., J. C. D., The Precept of Hearing Mass, XIV-188 pp., 1942.
159. GULCZYNSKI, REV. JOHN THEOPHILUS, J. C. D., The Desecration and Violation of Churches, X-126 pp., 1942.
160. HAMMILL, REV. JOHN LEO, M. A., J. C. D., The Obligations of the Traveler According to Canon 14, VIII-204 pp., 1942.
161. HAYDT, REV. JOHN JOSEPH, A. B., J. C. D., Reserved Benefices, XI-148 pp., 1942.
162. HUSER, REV. ROGER JOHN, O. F. M., A. B., J. C. D., The Crime of Abortion in Canon Law, XII-187 pp., 1942
163. KEARNEY, REV. FRANCIS PATRICK, A. B., S. T. L., J. C. D., The Principles of Canon 1127, X-162 pp., 1942.
164. LINAHEN, REV. LEO JAMES, S. T. L., J. C. D., De Absolutione Complicis in Peccato Turpi, V-114 pp., 1942.
165. MCCLOSKEY, REV. JOSEPH ALOYSIUS, A. B., J. C. D., The Subject of Ecclesiastical Law According to Canon 12, XVII-246 pp., 1942 (Printed 1943).
166. O'NEILL, REV. FRANCIS JOSEPH, C. SS. R., J. C. D., The Dismissal of Religious in Temporary Vows, VIII-220 pp., 1942.
167. PRINCE, REV. JOHN EDWARD, A. B., S. T. B., J. C. D., The Diocesan Chancellor, X-136 pp., 1942.
168. RIESNER, REV. ALBERT JOSEPH, C. SS. R., J. C. D., Apostates and Fugitives from Religious Institutes, IX-168 pp., 1942.
169. STENGER, REV. JOSEPH BERNARD, J. C. D., The Mortgaging of Church Property, 186 pp., 1942.

170. WALDRON, REV. JOSEPH FRANCIS, A. B., J. C. D., The Minister of Baptism, XII-197 pp., 1942.
171. WILLETT, REV. ROBERT ALBERT, J. C. D., The Probative Value of Documents in Ecclesiastical Trials, X-124 pp., 1942.
172. WOEBER, REV. EDWARD MARTIN, M. A., J. C. D., The Interpellations, XII-161 pp., 1942.
173. BENKO, REV. MATTHEW ALOYSIUS, O. S. B., M. A., J. C. D., The Abbot *Nullius,* XVI-148 pp., 1943.
174. CHRIST, REV. JOSEPH JAMES, M. A., S. T. L., J. C. D., Dispensation from Vindicative Penalties, XIV-285 pp., 1943.
175. CLANCY, REV. PATRICK M. J., O. P., A. B., S. T. LR., J. C. D., The Local Religious Superior, X-229 pp., 1943.
176. CLARKE, REV. THOMAS JAMES, J. C. D., Parish Societies, XII-147 pp., 1943.
177. CONNOLLY, REV. JOHN PATRICK, S. T. L., J. C. D., Synodal Examiners and Parish Priest Consultors, X-223 pp., 1943.
178. DRUMM, REV. WILLIAM MARTIN, A. B., J. C. D., Hospital Chaplains, XII-175 pp., 1943.
179. FLANAGAN, REV. BERNARD JOSEPH, A. B., S. T. L., J. C. D., The Canonical Erection of Religious Houses, X-147 pp., 1943.
180. KELLEHER, REV. STEPHEN JOSEPH, A. B., S. T. B., J. C. D., Discussions with Non-Catholics: Canonical Legislation, X-93 pp., 1943.
181. LEWIS, REV. GORDIAN, C. P., J. C. D., Chapters in Religious Institutes, XII-169 pp., 1943.
182. MARX, REV. ADOLPH, J. C. D., The Declaration of Nullity of Marriages Contracted Outside the Church, X-151 pp., 1943.
183. MATULENAS, REV. RAYMOND ANTHONY, O. S. B., A. B., J. C. D., Communication, a Source of Privileges, XII-225 pp., 1943.
184. O'LEARY, REV. CHARLES GERARD, C. SS. R., J. C. D., Religious Dismissed After Perpetual Profession, X-213 pp., 1943.
185. POWER, REV. CORNELIUS MICHAEL, J. C. D., The Blessing of Cemeteries, XII-231 pp., 1943.
186. SHUHLER, REV. RALPH VINCENT, O. S. A., J. C. D., Privileges of Religious to Absolve and Dispense, XII-195 pp., 1943.
187. ZIOLKOWSKI, REV. THADDEUS STANISLAUS, A. B., J. C. D., The Consecration and Blessing of Churches, XII-151 pp., 1943.
188. HENEGHAN, REV. JOHN JOSEPH, S. T. D., J. C. D., The Marriages of Unworthy Catholics: Canons 1065 and 1066, XVI-213 pp., 1944.
189. CARROLL, REV. COLEMAN FRANCIS, M. A., S. T. L., J. C. L., Charitable Institutions.
190. CIESLUK, REV. JOSEPH EDWARD, PH. B., S. T. L., J. C. D., National Parishes in the United States, VI-178 pp., 1944.
191. COBURN, REV. VINCENT PAUL, A. B., J. C. D., Marriages of Conscience, XII-172 pp., 1944.

192. CONNORS, REV. CHARLES PAUL, C. S. SP., A. B., J. C. D., Extra-Judicial Procurators in the Code of Canon Law, X-94 pp., 1944.
193. COYLE, REV. PAUL RAYMOND, A. B., J. C. D., Judicial Exceptions, X-142 pp., 1944.
194. FAIR, REV. BARTHOLOMEW FRANCIS, A. B., S. T. L., J. C. D., The Impediment of Abduction, XII-122 pp., 1944.
195. GALLAGHER, REV. THOMAS RAPHAEL, O. P., A. B., S. T. LR., J. C. D., The Examination of the Qualities of the Ordinand, X-166 pp., 1944.
196. GANNON, REV. JOHN MARK, S. T. L., J. C. D., The Interstices Required for the Promotion to Orders, XII-100 pp., 1944.
197. GOLDSMITH, REV. J. WILLIAM, B. C. S., S. T. L., J. C. D., The Competence of Church and State Over Marriages—Disputed Points, X-128 pp., 1944.
198. GOODWINE, REV. JOSEPH GERARD, A. B., S. T. B., J. C. D., The Reception of Converts, XIV-326 pp., 1944.
199. KOWALSKI, REV. ROMUALD EUGENE, O. F. M., A. B., J. C. D., Sustenance of Religious Houses of Regulars, X-174 pp., 1944.
200. MCCOY, REV. ALAN EDWARD, O. F. M., J. C. D., Force and Fear in Relation to Delictual Imputability and Penal Responsibility, XII-160 pp., 1944.
201. MCDEVITT, REV. VINCENT JOHN, PH. B., S. T. L., J. C. L., Perjury.
202. MARTIN, REV. THOMAS OWEN, PH. D., S. T. D., J. C. D., Adverse Possession, Prescription and Limitation of Actions: The Canonical "Praescriptio," XX-208 pp., 1944.
203. MIKLOSOVIC, REV. PAUL JOHN, A. B., J. C. L., Attempted Marriages and Their Consequent Juridic Effects.
204. MUNDY, REV. THOMAS MAURICE, A. B., S. T. L., J. C. D., The Union of Parishes, X-164 pp., 1944.
205. O'DEA, REV. JOHN COYLE, A. B., J. C. D., The Matrimonial Impediment of Nonage, VIII-126 pp., 1944.
206. OLALIA, REV. ALEXANDER AYSON, S. T. L., J. C. D., A Comparative Study of the Christian Constitution of States and the Constitution of the Philippine Commonwealth, XII-136 pp., 1944.
207. POISSON, REV. PIERRE-MARIE, C. S. C., A. B., PH. L., TH. L., J. C. L., Droits Patrimoniaux des Maisons et des Eglises Religieuses.
208. STADALNIKAS, REV. CASIMIR JOSEPH, M. I. C., J. C. D., Reservation of Censures, X-141 pp., 1944.
209. SULLIVAN, REV. EUGENE HENRY, S. T. L., J. C. D., Proof of the Reception of the Sacraments, X-165 pp., 1944.
210. VAUGHAN, REV. WILLIAM EDWARD, J. C. D., Constitutions for Diocesan Courts, X-210 pp., 1944.
211. PARO, REV. GINO, S. T. D., J. C. D., The Right of Papal Legation, X-221 pp., 1944 (Printed 1947).
212. BALZER, REV. RALPH FRANCIS, C. P., J. C. D., The Computation of Time in a Canonical Novitiate, X-227 pp., 1945.

213. DOUGHERTY, REV. JOHN WHELAN, A. B., S. T. L., J. C. D., De Inquisitione Speciali, XII-195 pp., 1945.
214. DZIOB, REV. MICHAEL WALTER, J. C. D., The Sacred Congregation for the Oriental Church, XII-181 pp., 1945.
215. EIDENSCHINK, REV. JOHN ALBERT, O. S. B., B. A., J. C. D., The Election of Bishops in the Letters of Pope Gregory the Great, VIII-200 pp., 1945.
216. GILL, REV. NICHOLAS, C. P., J. C. D., The Spiritual Prefect in Clerical Religious Houses of Study, X-140 pp., 1945.
217. HYNES, REV. HARRY GERARD, S. T. L., J. C. D., The Privileges of Cardinals, XII-183 pp., 1945.
218. MCDEVITT, REV. GERALD VINCENT, S. T. L., J. C. D., The Renunciation of an Ecclesiastical Office, XIV-179 pp., 1945.
219. MANNING, REV. JOSEPH LEROY, J. C. D., The Free Conferral of Offices, VII-116 pp., 1945.
220. MEYER, REV. LOUIS G., O. S. B., A. B., S. T. B., J. C. D., Alms-gathering by Religious, XII-163 pp., 1945.
221. O'DONNELL, REV. CLETUS FRANCIS, M. A., J. C. D., The Marriage of Minors, XII-268 pp., 1945.
222. PRUNSKIS, REV. JOSEPH, J. C. D., Comparative Law, Ecclesiastical and Civil, in Lithuanian Concordat, X-161 pp., 1945.
223. SWEENEY, REV. FRANCIS PATRICK, C. SS. R., J. C. D., The Reduction of Clerics to the Lay State, X-199 pp., 1945.
224. VOGELPOHL, REV. HENRY JOHN, J. C. D., The Simple Impediments to Holy Orders, XVI-190 pp., 1945.
225. BROCKHAUS, REV. THOMAS AQUINAS, O. S. B., J. C. D., Religious Who Are Known as *Conversi,* X-127 pp., 1945.
226. GRIESE, REV. ORVILLE NICHOLAS, S. T. D., J. C. D., The Marriage Contract and the Procreation of Offspring, XVI-224 pp., 1945.
227. BOUDREAUX, REV. WARREN LOUIS, J. C. D., The *"ab acatholicis nati"* of Canon 1099, § 2, XII-110 pp., 1946.
228. BOWE, REV. THOMAS JOSEPH, A. B., J. C. D., Religious Superioresses, VIII-206 pp., 1946.
229. DIEDERICHS, REV. MICHAEL FERDINAND, S. C. J., J. C. D., The Jurisdiction of the Latin Ordinaries over Their Oriental Subjects, XIV-153 pp., 1946.
230. DINGMAN, REV. MAURICE JOHN, A. B., S. T. L., J. C. L., The Plaintiff in Contentious Trials.
231. FRISON, REV. BASIL, C. M. F., M. MUS., J. C. D., The Retroactivity of Law, X-221 pp., 1946.
232. GALVIN, REV. WILLIAM ANTHONY, M. A., J. C. D., The Administrative Transfer of Pastors, XII-288 pp., 1946.
233. GORACY, REV. JOSEPH C., J. C. L., The Diriment Matrimonial Impediment of Major Orders.
234. HALE, REV. JOSEPH FRANCIS, M. A., S. T. L., J. C. D., The Pastor of Burial, X-247 pp., 1946 (Printed 1949).

235. HENRY, REV. JOSEPH ARTHUR, A. B., J. C. D., The Mass and Holy Communion: Interritual Law, XII-138 pp., 1946.

236. LINENBERGER, REV. HERBERT, C. PP. S., J. C. D., The False Denunciation of an Innocent Confessor, VIII-205 pp., 1946 (Printed 1949).

237. LOWRY, REV. JAMES MARTIN, A. B., J. C. D., Dispensation from Private Vows, XII-266 pp., 1946.

238. LYNCH, REV. GEORGE EDWARD, A. B., S. T. L., J. C. D., Coadjutors and Auxiliaries of Bishops, X-107 pp., 1946 (Printed 1947).

239. LYNCH, REV. TIMOTHY, M. S. SS. T., J. C. D., Contracts between Bishops and Religious Congregations, XIII-232 pp., 1946.

240. MCCLUNN, REV. JUSTIN DAVID, A. B., S. T. L., J. C. D., Administrative Recourse, VII-142 pp., 1946.

241. LOHMULLER, REV. MARTIN NICHOLAS, A. B., J. C. D., The Promulgation of Law, XII-140 pp., 1947.

242. MCGRATH, REV. JAMES, A. B., J. C. D., The Privilege of the Canon, XII-156 pp., 1946.

243. MARBACH, REV. JOSEPH FRANCIS, A. B., J. C. D., Marriage Legislation for the Catholics of the Oriental Rites in the United States and Canada, XIV-314 pp., 1946.

244. SHIMKUS, REV. BERNARD ALOYSIUS, A. B., J. C. L., The Determination and Transfer of Rite.

245. SMITH, REV. VINCENT MICHAEL, A. B., S. T. L., J. C. L., Ignorance Affecting Matrimonial Consent.

246. WACHTRLE, REV. PAUL ANTHONY, A. B., J. C. L., The Baptism of the Children of Non-Catholics.

247. CROTTY, REV. MATTHEW M., J. C. D., The Recipient of First Holy Communion, X-142 pp., 1947.

248. EAGLÊTON, REV. GEORGE, J. C. D., The Quinquennial Faculties, Formula IV, XIV-199 pp., 1947 (Printed 1948).

249. GIBBONS, REV. MARION L., C. M., LL. B., J. C. D., Domicile of the Wife Unlawfully Separated from Her Husband, XIV-171 pp., 1947.

250. KELLY, REV. BERNARD M., S. T. L., J. C. D., The Functions Reserved to Pastors, IX-141 pp., 1947.

251. KILCULLEN, REV. THOMAS J., LL. M., J. C. D., The Collegiate Moral Person as Party Litigant, X-150 pp., 1947.

252. LAFONTAINE, REV. GERMAIN J., W. F., J. C. D., Relations Canoniques entre Le Missionnaire et Ses Superieurs, X-117 pp., 1947.

253. LANE, REV. LORAS T., A. B., S. T. L., J. C. D., Matrimonial Procedure in the Ordinary Court of Second Instance, XVI-184 pp., 1947.

254. LOVER, REV. JAMES F., C. SS. R., J. C. D., The Master of Novices, X-168 pp., 1947.

255. MCNICHOLAS, REV. TIMOTHY J., J. C. L., The *Septimae Manus* Witness.

256. MAROSITZ, REV. JOSEPH J., M. S. C., J. C. D., Obligations and Privileges of Religious Promoted to the Episcopal or Cardinalitial Dignities, XII-180 pp., 1947.

257. MURPHY, REV. FRANCIS J., A. B., J. C. D., Legislative Powers of the Provincial Council, XII-158 pp., 1947.
258. O'BRIEN, REV. ROMAEUS W., O. CARM., J. C. D., The Provincial Superior in Religious Orders of Men, X-294 pp., 1947.
259. PFALLER, REV. BENEDICT A., O. S. B., J. C. D., The *Ipso Facto* Effected Dismissal of Religious, XII-225 pp., 1947.
260. POPEK, REV. ALPHONSE S., M. A., J. C. D., The Rights and Obligations of Metropolitans, XX-460 pp., 1947.
261. RISTUCCIA, REV. BERNARD J., C. M., J. C. D., Quasi-Religious, XVI-318 pp., 1947 (Printed 1949).
262. SONNTAG, REV. NATHANIEL L., O. F. M. CAP., J. C. D., Censorship of Special Classes of Books, XII-147 pp., 1947.
263. STADLER, REV. JOSEPH N., J. C. D., Frequent Holy Communion, X-158 pp., 1947.
264. SZAL, REV. IGNATIUS J., J. C. D., The Communication of Catholics with Schismatics, XII-217 pp., 1947.
265. WAGNER, REV. URBAN S., O. F. M. CONV., J. C. D., Parochial Substitute Vicars and Supplying Priests, IX-126 pp., 1947.
266. QUINN, REV. JOSEPH, M. A., J. C. D., Documents Required for the Reception of Orders, XII-207 pp., 1948.
267. BENNINGTON, REV. JAMES CLEMENT, A. B., J. C. L., The Recipient of Confirmation.
268. BLAHER, REV. DAMIAN JOSEPH, O. F. M., A. B., J. C. L., The Ordinary Processes in Causes of Beatification and Canonization.
269. CLUNE, REV. ROBERT BELL, B. A., J. C. L., The Judicial Interrogation of the Parties.
270. COURTEMANCHE, REV. BASIL F., B. A., J. C. L., The Total Simulation of Matrimonial Consent.
271. DLOUHY, REV. MAUR JOHN, O. S. B., A. B., J. C. L., The Ordination of Exempt Religious.
272. DONOVAN, REV. JOHN THOMAS, PH. B., S. T. L., J. C. D., The Clerical Obligations of Canons 138 and 140, XII-209 pp., 1948.
273. FREKING, REV. FREDERICK W., A. B., S. T. B., J. C. L., The Canonical Installation of Pastors.
274. FULTON, REV. THOMAS B., J. C. L., Prenuptial Investigation.
275. GODLEY, REV. JAMES P., J. C. L., The Time and the Place for the Celebration of Mass.
276. KANE, REV. THOMAS A., A. B., B. S., J. C. D., The Jurisdiction of the Patriarchs of the Major Sees in Antiquity and in the Middle Ages, XII-111 pp., 1948 (Printed 1949).
277. KENNEDY, REV. ANDREW A., J. C. L., The Annual Pastoral Report to the Local Ordinary.
278. KONRAD, REV. JOSEPH GEORGE, J. C. L., Transfer of Religious.
279. KRESS, REV. ALPHONSE, J. C. L., Contumacy in Ecclesiastical Trials.

280. McCartney, Rev. Marcellus Anthony, O. F. M., M. A., J. C. L., Faculties of Regular Confessors.
281. McCaslin, Rev. Edward Patrick, M. A., S. T. L., J. C. L., The Division of Parishes.
282. McElroy, Rev. Francis J., A. B., J. C. L., The Privileges of Bishops.
283. Quinn, Rev. Stephen, M. S. SS. T., J. C. D., Relation between the Local Ordinary and Religious of Diocesan Approval, XII-153 pp., 1948 (Printed 1949).
284. Schneider, Rev. Edelhard Louis, A. D. S., M. A., J. C. D., The Status of Secularized Ex-Religious Clerics, X-155 pp., 1948.
285. Thompson, Rev. Chester J., A. B., J. C. L., The Simple Removal from Office.
286. O'Brien, Rev. Kenneth R., A. B., J. C. D., The Nature of Support of Diocesan Priests in the United States, XVI-162 pp., 1949.
287. Metz, Rev. John E., S. T. L., J. C. D., The Recording Judge in the Ecclesiastical Collegiate Tribunal, X-130 pp., 1949.
288. Reinhardt, Rev. Marion J., S. T. L., J. C. L., The Rogatory Commission.
289. Ortega-Uhink, Rev. Juan, S. J., J. C. L., De Delicto Sollicitationis.
290. Casey, Rev. James V., J. C. L., A Study of Canon 2222, § 1.
291. Allgeier, Rev. Joseph L., J. C. L., The Canonical Obligation of Preaching in Parish Churches.
292. Cahill, Rev. Daniel R., J. C. L., The Custody of the Holy Eucharist.
293. Carr, Rev. Aidan, O. F. M. Conv., S. T. D., J. C. L., Vocation to the Priesthood: Its Canonical Concept.
294. Knopke, Rev. Roch F., O. F. M., J. C. L., Reverential Fear in Matrimonial Cases in Asiatic Countries: Rota Cases.
295. Lavelle, Rev. Howard D., J. C. L., The Obligation of Holding Sacred Missions in Parishes.
296. Mickells, Rev. Anthony B., J. C. L., The Constitutive Elements of Parishes.
297. Noone, Rev. John J., J. C. L., Nullity in Judicial Acts.
298. Sheehan, Rev. Daniel E., J. C. L., The Minister of Holy Communion.
299. Statkus, Rev. Francis J., J. C. L., The Minister of the Last Sacraments.
300. Cook, Rev. John P., J. C. L., Ecclesiastical Communities and Their Ability to Induce Legal Customs.
301. Fazzalaro, Rev. Francis J., J. C. L., The Place for the Hearing of Confessions.
302. Hannan, Rev. Philip M., J. C. L., The Canonical Concept of *congrua sustentatio* for the Secular Clergy.
303. Quinn, Rev. Hugh G., S. T. L., J. C. L., The Particular Penal Precept.
304. Gallagher, Rev. John F., J. C. L., The Matrimonial Impediment of Public Propriety.
305. Welsh, Rev. Thomas J., J. C. L., The Use of the Portable Altar.

www.ingramcontent.com/pod-product-compliance
Lightning Source LLC
LaVergne TN
LVHW050221080826
844660LV00012B/450

* 9 7 8 0 8 1 3 2 2 4 7 7 0 *